Cor

Common Sense For The Soul

Guidelines For Life A - Z

Patricia Lite Hickman

ISBN : 1-4196-0117-2

To order additional copies, please contact us.
BookSurge, LLC
www.booksurge.com
1-866-308-6235
orders@booksurge.com

Common Sense For The Soul

CHAPTERS A to Z

ACKNOWLEDGMENTS

A heartfelt Thank You for permission to quote or for teaching me what I needed to learn goes to:

Erma Bombeck
Joan Borysenko, Ph.D., Fire in the Soul
http://joanborysenko.com/html/bio.html
David Cameron, CEO
http://www.imagesofone.com
Patricia Diane Cota-Robles
http://www.1spirit.com/eraofpeace
Charles Fillmore, founder of Unity
(also known as Unity School of Christianity)
http://science.gcc.edu/reli/kemeny/new_page_19.html
Benjamin Franklin
Julia Havey
http://www.weightlossbyjulia.com/
Dennis P. O'Hara D.C.
http://www.chirosense.com.

FOREWORD

Becoming a strong person is a choice, often it is a necessity. Life has many winding curves and we can find ourselves in a place of weakness, in the place of a victim, someone who views the world with a "poor me" attitude. We can see and feel so much pain, we get stuck in sadness. Not knowing any better, (sometimes we don't even realize we are doing it) we can wind up giving our power away, either to a partner, friend or spouse. We can enhance our relationships by bringing our strengths into them and merging with the strength of another. It all boils down to whether we want to be sick, tired and depressed, or vibrantly healthy, happy and strong. These pages will give you tips, and some tools, as you journey through the classroom of life.

Life is the classroom for the soul, we all go through cycles, change, and growth. With each birthday, our "personal year" changes and brings its own special challenges, change, growth, opportunity to set goals and the ability to win. The greatest relief? finding the connection and resonating your spirit with that of the Great Spirit, Higher Power, Allah, God, Creator, Goddess, (whatever name you call your Spiritual Deity).

The single most important thing you can do for yourself, is to LOVE yourself. Bless yourself daily by affirming: "I bless you for the Divinity within you.

The single most important thing you can do for your child, your relative, or your friends, is to teach or show them how special they are, and to love them unconditionally.

The most important lesson? Love, including love of the self.

The greatest asset? HAPPINESS! If you don't feel happy 50% of the time, take the time to learn the "Skill of Happiness". It is true that half of our happiness comes from other people or outer circumstances, but the other half, comes from within. If we do not feel happy within, we will not know true happiness. Open your eyes toward the Heavens and let your light shine.

There is a Christian Children's Song, the chorus is: "This Little Light Of Mine, I'm gonna let it shine, let it shine, let it shine, LET IT SHINE". So, Dear One,,, let it shine!

It is my hope that these pages will Bless you and help you shine, not only towards others, but within.

INTRODUCTION

I am a strong woman. I did not become strong overnight, it took 30 something years before I began to realize that I really might be stronger than I thought. I appeared to others as strong most of my life, (I put on a confident front). As a child, the abandonment by our parents taught me to *stuff* hurt feelings, when all I wanted to do was cry. It wasn't until age 45 that I felt confident in saying, "yes, I am a strong woman".

What I learned came through trial and error, and a few bumps, or lumps in the school of life, or was that "the school of hard knocks" (soft smile) I like to say: "I prayed for Wisdom, boy, did I get it!"

I was born into a Roman Catholic family, attending parochial school. Mass everyday before school, for 8 years, taught me about Angels, God and how to pray. I have since learned that God has many names. My local Unity Church has on their billboard: "Many paths, one God"

My search for the right Spiritual Path, taught me that prayer or blessing is very powerful. I came to know and understand that I (we), have many guides, in the physical world as well as the Spiritual Realm. Some of us call them Guides, some of us call them Angels. I have developed a personal relationship with Angels. I can truly say what I have learned is how to be happy in a life that doesn't always make sense.

*To my son, Kevin, twin daughter's Kelley (Craig) and Kathleen (Michael). To all of my wonderful Grandchildren: Davonte, Kae'Leen, Kevin, Qwavon, Nicholas, Katelynn, D'Andre, Mikaelynn, and Endia. My children can still bless me with other grandchildren and they are included here, before I meet them! You all helped me to grow up, taught me about loving unconditionally, and have been the greatest blessings in my life. My grandchildren helped me to see the parts I have *right* and the things I still have to learn. What a special honor to know and love all of you! This guide is my gift and blessing in case you ever ask the question "What should I do"? I love you all!*

*I am forever indebted to the Guard family, for sharing their strength and unconditional love. *Mom* Juanita Guard, is THE most beautiful, 70 something, strongest woman I know! She has faced heaven, hell and all kinds of trauma in between, and is a beautiful, strong, Christian woman!*

A special thanks to my brother Michael, and Barbara, for supporting this work and for the entry in Chapter X. To my girlfriends, Janice, Gail, Patricia and Dinah, other friends, and loved ones, for the friendship and growth!

A great big THANK YOU, to Anne, and Coni, for help and motivation. A huge THANK YOU to Las and Suzann for editing this work. Melanie "thank you" seems so insignificant, the truth is, without you, this book might not have made it out of my document file!

To the thousands of wonderful clients I have spent time with over the years! It was in teaching you that I became aware of how useful guidelines could be when a person comes face to face with life changes.

To my Sisters and Brothers in Spirit. May you continue to search for the right path for you, one that will help you to realize and know the Divine Spirit within (and freely share your knowledge with others). My prayer is that these pages will serve to point the way.

CHAPTER A

Abandonment, Abortion, Abuse, Achieving Goals, Addiction, Affairs, Affirmations, Aging, Ambition, Ancestors, Angels, Anger, Anxiety, Apologize, Apples, Astrology, Attitude, Aura

ABANDONMENT: I consider abandonment silent abuse. A child abandoned by one or both of their parents can take many years to recover, (if they do); so much depends on who became their caretaker afterwards; whether or not they were loving is very important to the emotional development of the child. If the caretaker felt that raising someone else's child was a burden, all hell can break loose in the emotional development of the child.

Single Parenthood is very common now and many of these children were abandoned by at least one parent. When children process the break up of their parents, they can easily decide that there was something about them that was wrong OR unlovable since the parent did not stay with her/him. They need double the love from the parent left to raise them. If they do not get that, they can wind up self sabotaging for a lifetime.

Fortunate are those who recover and live a normal life, which is possible for all of them, unless the abandonment and lack of love sets them up for severe mental illness. Abandonment at any age can be a disaster, but the more mature a person is, the stronger their faith and belief in a Higher Power, or Diety, the more willing to seek therapy and talk openly about it, the easier it is to overcome the wounds and heartache abandonment leaves in its wake.

We get many opportunities to heal wounds and can choose

to just "stuff" the pain away and get busy with life. If we do not get counseling early on, the wounds might not heal until midlife, between the ages of 42- 45. That seems to be when we get the forgiveness and healing lessons right.

Not too many of those who have been abandoned get an apology from the other party(s), the bottom line to healing abandonment is forgiveness. If you find that difficult, consider the fact that if you had of been in that person's shoes, with the emotional baggage they were carrying, you might be compelled to do the same thing, given the same set of circumstances.

An excellent way for you to give yourself closure is to write a letter to that person, explaining just how you feel; how the abandonment hurt you and how you have not been dealing with it well; get all feelings written down that come to mind. Since you cannot mail or give them the letter, burn it; while it is burning, take some deep breathes; when you let the breathe go, let the pain you just wrote about go with it; do at least 10 of these cleansing breaths; once the letter is burned, do the forgiveness mantra:

I FULLY AND FREELY FORGIVE YOU, I LOOSE YOU AND LET YOU GO, ON YOUR WAY NOW TO YOUR HIGHEST GOOD AS I GO ON TO MINE. It is done, It is done, It is DONE! (Metaphysical law of Decree, 3 times).Take a deep breath and affirm: "Today is the first day of the rest of my life".

The loss of a loved one through death, can leave one feeling like they have been abandoned. Is that *wrong*? No! When it comes to grief, there is no right or wrong. We are all unique in how we handle grief, some recover quicker than others but our feelings are part of the human condition. An excellent affirmation:

MY LIFE AND AFFAIRS ARE IN DIVINE ORDER.

Grief counseling can help, you may also want to put some closure on your feelings of hurt and abandonment by doing the closure technique mentioned above; do allow yourself to grieve and do not be afraid of the stages of grief; just understand as you recognize each stage that it is okay for you to feel these things and it will pass. See Chapters F—Forgiveness, G—Grief.

ABORTION: This is a touchy subject, an emotional and personal one. It is the author's personal opinion that abortion isn't the best option, with the exception of life threatening illness to the child or mother. To me, "life threatening" can also mean a total devastation of the spirit which can lead to permanent mental illness. I favor early abortion if that is the option one chooses. The pain and undeserved abuse an unwanted child can be forced to live is something they will carry with them and suffer from for a lifetime. Abortion is a personal experience between the parent(s) and family, the whole ordeal can be very painful for the mother, (and the father too, if he isn't the one pushing for the abortion), not only during the experience, but later on.

I feel that more extensive counseling than what is offered by abortion clinics is best and counseling after the abortion is also a good idea. Abortion as we know it in these times is a personal choice. Do consider the fact that your circumstances can and most likely will change in the future.

If one chooses an abortion, then be prepared for emotional memories triggered by nearly anything, at any time, in the future. If you make this decision, then be committed that this is the ONLY solution available to you and your family to cope with an unwanted pregnancy; forgive yourself, and when you do remember it, forgive yourself again. You did the best you could do under the circumstances, even if it seems selfish to you later on; even if others callously tell you that it was selfish.

The good news is that when we learn better, we do better, and applies to this decision too. Should you choose to have an abortion, hopefully, you will have a loved one or trusted friend to be at your side, and not have to go through this experience alone.

If you are facing this on your own, know that you are a survivor and this too, shall pass. There will be brighter days ahead, life is full of many "Hello's and Goodbyes".

If the abortion is someone else's idea, and not yours, and

you do not want it, then do **not** do it, not only will you feel guilty later, but you can wind up hating the other person for forcing you to do something you do not want to do. In the case of a parent insisting that their child has an abortion, statistics have proven that many girls or women who abort a pregnancy will get pregnant soon afterwards. Most likely the parent is attempting to make the best decision for the child they love; although sometimes that decision has roots in selfishness and turns out to not be the best thing for the pregnant girl, but again I say, they are doing the best they know how to at that time and forgiveness work will be in order. Real honest communication is required so as to not destroy the family bonds of love. When we know better, we do better.

The violent demonstrations at abortion clinics are very out of line and should be stopped. My grandmother taught me that " two wrongs don't make a right." For many years abortions were performed by back street butcher types and the damage done often horrendous and permanent.

If the pregnancy is due to a rape situation, that is what I call a "double whammy" and will require you to think carefully about the abortion on different levels, it may be the best thing to do, unless you are VERY mentally committed that the child born of this situation will not suffer from your feelings about the rape later on.

A child conceived from a rape had nothing whatsoever to do with what happened to you. I personally knew a mother, who would quickly tell everyone she met (in front of the child) that he was conceived because of a rape. Saying such things can place a terrible burden on the child, please consider that.

There are many birth control options available, find one that is right for you before a pregnancy happens. There have been many women who were told by a medical doctor they could not conceive, and then they did. Abortion shouldn't be used as a form of birth control. There is now a "morning after" pill, which would be well worth exploring with your physician well ahead of the time you might need it, what I am saying is "be prepared"!

It often happens in early sexual experience, that young girls are too embarrassed to push for the use of condoms. I've also heard older women say they are too embarrassed. If you find that you are too embarrassed to discuss this, then you are either too young to be having the experience and/or old enough to get over the embarrassment and protect yourself. Think about your decision to become sexually active with someone, then practice in your mirror first, talking about the use of condoms so that you know ahead of time what you to say. The best way of course, is straight up: "I cannot have sex (or make love) with you if you do not use a condom". Even if its 3 months down the road, use the condom until you are married not only to prevent pregnancy but to at least attempt to protect yourself against sexually transmitted disease.

A word of caution: condoms do break or are put on, or taken off wrong which can still result in pregnancy or disease, but it is still better than doing nothing about protecting yourself. You cannot look at a person and tell that they are carrying a sexually transmitted disease (STD) some disease such as herpes last forever, in the case of aides it will result in death sometimes quickly, sometimes not, but always painful.

ABUSE: There are many forms of abuse, the most life threatening of course, is physical abuse, but mental abuse wounds the spirit. Abuse can take any form, emotional, verbal, silent (when your loved one doesn't speak to you for days on end, or just walks out of your life). Temper tantrums, where everything but the kitchen sink gets thrown around, kicked, punched or broken.

No one DESERVES abuse. It is time that we commit to stamping out abuse within our homes, families and lives. Change begins with the "man in the mirror" a song that should be learned by all. It is time for parents and schools to get a tight reign on the children. Who among us wasn't taunted by kids at school or in the neighborhood? Teach tolerance in the home and schools will not be such a hard place.

Teach tolerance in the schools as part of the health curriculum, send handouts home with the children and the whole family will benefit. If enough parents request their schools develop such a program, it will make a big difference in the cruelty children inflict on their peers. The taunting by other kids is often remembered for a lifetime.

I have heard many women say that their boyfriend or husband is *just* verbally, or *just* emotionally abusive. Hateful words or statements and name calling flashback in the minds and memory of the person it was said to, even after the person who said them is no longer around, or even if you cannot remember their names, you will remember what was said. I believe that such treatment is to be considered bona fide abuse and should not be tolerated or minimized as *just*.

We live with abuse, for many reasons, dependency on the abuser, and fear are the two main reasons. Fear of being alone or fear of our ability to put a better life together; fear that if you report the abuser or get away from them, they will kill you.

Fear and abuse are related; one person lives in fear, the other abuses. Many are afraid that they are unable to "make it" on their own. That is really not the truth.

Too often, the abuser convinces the victim that it is all their fault; the victim of abuse suffers from low self esteem and sometimes will feel that they deserve the abuse they are getting; It is not the truth.

It is important to a), take your power back, and get out of the situation. b), learn how powerful, important and sacred, you actually are. The time to think about abuse is before it happens. How do you feel about it? How will you react to it? Dr. Phil says: "We teach people how to treat us". That is a true statement; If you tolerate abuse from others, you have taught them that it is okay to abuse you. One common misconception is that if the person is given enough love, they will stop abusing; again, this is simply not the truth. We tend to feel that love can change a person, it doesn't; it can enhance who they are, but if they are a bully, they do not know how to accept the love one tries to give them so it barely makes a dent in the armour of meanness they use to protect themselves.

There is many a sorry wife who became a bride thinking

that marriage would change her man's rough edges; then found that marriage became a prison of misery not only for her, but also for children born of the marriage, or taken into it. It might be many years if ever before the ordeal is over.

If you are involved with a person who abuses you emotionally or physically, consider that life can be very peaceful without them. Too many women feel that they must stay in an abusive situation because they cannot support themselves. If you are in that situation I suggest getting some counseling, get healthy, if necessary get a job, or discover your talents and start your own business and move out. See Chapter S—Self Esteem.

There are many insidious forms of abuse. An abusive parent, while they might not physically harm their child, can be guilty of what I call, "tone of voice abuse. " When they speak at, instead of to, their children; constant yelling at children will change who they are. Once they are adults, they will have to live with (so will other people), the job you did in parenting, so do it well. You will also have to live with the job you did, guilt can be a sadness that will stay with you for the rest of your life. If you feel that you are abusing your children, get some help. Every major city has some resources available. One web source is this: http://www.parentsanonymous.org

Parents Anonymous has groups all over the United States. It only takes one person to make up their minds to stop abuse in the family to break the vicious cycle of abuse.

One thing is for sure, abused children, can become abusive adults. They do not *have to* become an abuser if they were abused. All abused children do not grow up to be abusers for the simple reason that they make a conscious choice not to abuse and then follow through with therapy and/or their own treatment plan. If there is no therapy, no conscious choice (which will still include some therapy and forgiveness work) then more often than not, the abused child will abuse their own children, even if they think "I'll never do that to my child".

There is no excuse for harsh communication, even if you, "mean well," that includes sarcastic comments or phrases. We are in control of what comes out of our mouths.

Self-abuse is prominent in our society, if others abuse us, we will eventually abuse ourselves, i.e., "I'm so stupid" and the host of other negatives we attach to ourselves. For too many generations people have abused themselves with everything from self-hatred and mutilation, to simply not bathing and keeping the body or their home clean.

If you recognize abuse in your life, and that includes not taking proper care of yourself, or not wanting to, seek therapy to help you put your life in order.

The Golden Rule applies to abuse: "Do unto others as you would have them to do you". If you don't like getting hit, don't hit! Often we see young people hitting each other and they say they are just *playing*. It is my opinion that hitting is not an acceptable form of playing or showing affection.

When someone doesn't get enough love in their life especially while they are very young, they can, and often do, become abusive. Sometimes abuse is a way of life for the family. Family members talk to each other gruff and abusively, or worse, curse each other. The cycle can be broken by one person saying: "No More" and meaning it. From that point on it is a learning process. Write out what treatment you want from others, and what treatment you expect to give to those around you. A good affirmation: "I am loved and loving". Invite the Angels of love to be in your homes. Where Angels hang out there is joy. See Chapter A—Affirmations and Angels.

Everyone puts his or her best foot forward in dating. We cannot know, the wonderful person we just met might turn into our worst nightmare, until we've known them for several months, or in some sad cases, years.

There will be signs of a potential abuser early on, as in the first 6 weeks, but clear warnings by the end of 90 days; that's not to long to wait to fall in love is it? If signs of abuse start, don't be so in love that you think your love will change that person. It usually doesn't and even if it might, that could be many bruises down the road. If you meet someone and they are "playfully" hitting, or wrestling as a way to have "fun", that is an indication they might become a physical abuser later. Some fellas will test you by wrestling around just to get an idea of how strong you are.

If someone is always teasing hurtfully and then say they are "just kidding" that is a strong indication they probably are or will become an emotional abuser. If that wonderful guy or gal you just met seems to have a temper or angers easily, gets a flat and hits the car, there could be trouble ahead, proceed with caution.

Don't be afraid on the 1st few dates, to let it be known that you dial 911 any time you are hit or abused, then mean it. Of course, you first must have an agreement with yourself that you will not tolerate being abused.

If you are reading this right now, and live in a physically abusive situation, please be strong enough to get out of the relationship; contact an agency to get some help and ask for a number to a woman's shelter or hotline. Get started with counseling, you will soon find that you are able to get out on your own and take care of yourself perfectly well and in peace.

There are many fine people in the world that will not abuse you and most of all, no matter what the person abusing you says, you DO NOT deserve this, No one should tolerate abuse, clearly, no one should have to. See Chapters B—Banish, D—Dysfunctional

ACHIEVING GOALS: Believe it! **A**chieve it! If you feel that you can do something, you can; if you believe that you cannot, you won't. It's as simple as that.

How to Achieve Your Goals Effortlessly, Guaranteed -Can you really achieve your money, health, relationship and other goals effortlessly or do you have to struggle? Can you move in a way that guarantees that your goals are achieved, or are you at the mercy of luck?

Yes, you can achieve your goals effortlessly. As much as your logical mind may tell you that effortless goal achievement is impossible, that is still a conditioned belief. For evidence, look to nature. How do you suppose a tiny seed grows into a giant tree with no construction workers supervising the building of that tree? How do you suppose you grew without any effort on your part from a tiny egg and sperm into a full grown being? Yes, you ate, but you didn't have to do anything to grow. How do you suppose this entire planet has sustained itself for millions and millions of years without any trucks coming in from outer space with food and material deliveries? Nature, by nature, moves forward effortlessly.

Have you ever observed the ocean's waves crashing at a beach? Do you know how much electricity and technology, work and money, would have to go into a machine that would replicate that if we were to build one? Yet nature creates crashing ocean waves the world over for your enjoyment, free, and without any effort on the part of the ocean. Simply by being an ocean, and working with the laws of the universe, tremendous power is released effortlessly.

And that brings us to the part about the guarantee. Yes, your goals can be achieved in a guaranteed way. The amazing thing about the universe is that it is an organized place. The whole of it is one big miracle! And what keeps it going is what you may call laws of the universe. Now, these laws never err even once (you can imagine what a disaster that would be if they did).

So here is how your guarantee comes in: If you flow against these laws, then you have to struggle to achieve anything. If you flow with the laws, then, by nature, you enter effortlessness. See Chapter T—Thought. Now we shall look at the one law that we need to know about for effortless achievement of your goals. This is the Law of Attraction. Scientifically, you may think of it as harmony, like in music.

Sounds that are of a matching frequency and wavelength will resonate and create harmony. They build upon each other. In fact, they activate each other. When you strike a pitching fork when in a silent room, any object that would resonate with the sound coming from that tuning fork will begin to vibrate and hum in resonance! Do you see the science behind that? Like energy attracts and builds, unlike energy repels and destroys. OK, now let us look at something else. In the above example, it must have occurred to you that it is the vibration from the tuning fork that activated other objects in the room to vibrate as well. Vibration. That is the key.

Everything in this universe is made of energy. In fact, it is not made of energy, it is energy. It is only your five senses that trick you into seeing forms. Forms are simply the brain's interpretation of various energy activities. Now, all energy vibrates. You vibrate. In fact, you are like a giant transmitter and receiver, always sending out and receiving frequencies. That is why you hear a cheap radio crackle with interference when you walk near the antennae. So let us get that settled. You vibrate, and that vibration rate changes.

For example, when you are happy, you vibrate faster and you feel lighter. And vice versa. In fact, everything becomes lighter as it increases its vibration (think of ice becoming water and then steam through the action of heating and thus raising vibration). So you vibrate and so does everything else. So what? Simple. Let us quickly review.

1. Vibration is in everything, including you and the things you desire in your goals.

2. Like vibration matches, attracts, and builds. Unlike vibration repels and destroys.

3. This is a Universal Law that never once decides to act otherwise. You can call it the Law of Attraction. It is based on the scientific working of energy, the stuff we and everything else is. Therefore, to get or achieve something, match yourself with its vibration. How do you know what your vibration is? You know by what you feel. Your feelings are your indicator of your vibration. And your imagination, your thoughts, activates your feelings.

To get or achieve something, match yourself with its vibration. And your imagination, your thoughts, activates your feelings. Let us see exactly how that is done. These steps can be expanded for more accuracy, but the following quick summary will get you started very well.

1. First, decide what your goal is. For this example, let us assume that your goal is to have a new car. Write that down. It is

very important that you write it down, as that crystallizes your thoughts and gives a boost to the manifestation process.

2. Next, get some pictures that are similar to the end result of your goals. You will use these to help you imagine, visualize, and therefore match your vibration to your achieved goal and therefore make it happen. For example, if you wish to have a new car, get some pictures of the type of car you would like. You can get those free off the Internet. If you know exactly which model of a car you would like, get pictures of that model.

3. Now it is time to program your conscious and subconscious mind, and your emotions, so that they all match your goal. In our new car example, take some quiet time to familiarize yourself with how it would feel like to actually have this new car. First of all, clearly write down the features you would like in this new car. We shall call this the form. Now, even more importantly, write down the feelings you expect to get from this new car. Include feelings, sights, sounds, tastes, smells, and touch. Also write down the benefits you expect to get from this car, and the reasons why you desire this new car. We shall call this the essence.

4. In your mind, combine the form and the essence, and the pictures you collected. The idea is to familiarize your conscious and unconscious mind, and your emotions, with the total feelings of having achieved your goal already. Close your eyes and just imagine yourself at the point just after you achieve your goal. Run that movie in your mind's eye, including all aspects of form and essence. Do this 10, 20 or even 100 times, as many as you feel is necessary until it feels natural to you? It should feel like the next natural step is for it to actually happen. Once you capture the totality of that feeling, you have got yourself a matching vibration to your goal.

5. Next, clear yourself of any vibrations that contradict your goal. You cannot achieve a goal if you vibrate against it. For example, a contrary vibration is disbelief or a feeling that you are not worthy or capable of achieving such a goal.

6. Once you have your matching vibration and have eliminated contradicting vibrations, you are done. Whenever

you think of your goal, bring up the total feeling. Whenever a contrary feeling comes up, gently let it go (do not engage it) and bring up the matching feeling.

7. Detach yourself from two things: time and form. The universe delivers by essence primarily. The feeling you put out, the essence, is what will come back. In other words, the solution that will be brought to you will bring you the essence you held when you were visualizing your goal. Sometimes that form may be the exact one you had in mind, sometimes it will be different. Just know two things: the Universe always delivers, but in its infinite intelligence it delivers in the form most suitable to the essence it received. What does this mean to you? Well, for one, do not insist that your new car will come through any particular sequence of steps, or from your income and savings, or from a particular shop, and so on.

Do not insist on the particular car (form). Do not insist on the timing. You do not know what the most efficient delivery is. Your view is definitely more limited than that of the universe. Any insisting will only mess with the vibration (you will feel disappointed because you will have judged yourself so based on your insisting). Let go. Detach yourself from form and time. For certain, a form that accurately matches the essence you put out will be delivered to you. That is guaranteed. Let go, detach, as if it didn't matter. Let go of that feeling of neediness.

8. Act when called upon. As you go about your life, certain things and people will come your way. This is the universe orchestrating a Synchronicity of events that will lead to your goal being achieved. Stay present and alert. When these come, act upon them. Remember always to be detached. Act purely for the sake of acting, not insisting on a particular outcome. You will find yourself miraculously having achieved your goal, out of the blue, step-by-step, in a most amazing way that you could not possibly have planned for! It is very true that you can have anything if you believe it. But remember, if you are having trouble finding your faith, simply look instead at the system, and you will see that faith is not even necessary, once you know that the system has been created by the Creator to work perfectly all

the time, regardless. What you put in is what you get out. Your job, then, is simply not to think against yourself, and as long as you do not think against yourself, all your desires will naturally manifest. I wish you the highest possible achievements.

If you wish to know more about all this, see http: //www.imagesofone.com/. Article written by David Cameron, CEO ImagesOfOne.com, author of Raising Humans and A. Happy Pocket Full of Money, and developer of the Prova Life Goals Effortless Achiever+ and Prova Life Map Numerology software. These and titles such as Think and Grow Rich, As A Man Thinketh, and more are available for download and free trial.

ADDICTION: We can become addicted to almost anything! An addiction sneaks up on you, and does not discriminate against gender, race, creed, or culture, all humans (even animals) can become addicted to something at any time in ones life. Addictions do not discriminate by age, although we like to say "the older you are, the wiser" that does not hold true with addictions.

Fact is, addictions run in families. Christian, and Pentecostal people believe that it is an "Ancestral Curse," it certainly is true that it can repeat for many generations until each individual chooses to manage addictive behavior. It is never cured, but it certainly can be managed.

You probably will not be introduced to an addiction by a stranger. Usually it will be someone you know, like or love. Once addicted, it isn't until you are ready to look at how the addiction is causing your life to feel painful, that you can recover from it.

The bottom line to healing any addiction is that you have to first identify it, and then want to control it bad enough that you will stop using or doing whatever is harming you. Denial is a big part of the addiction process. Lying to one's self and others sets one up for yet more challenges with the addiction. Dr. Phil says: "You can't fix what you don't acknowledge", I very much agree with that, although I like to say, "Awareness is half the battle won, but you still have to win the war."

We are now recognizing "hard" addictions and "soft"

addictions; that includes controlling or even helping others, food, talking on the phone, wasting too much time on the computer or other game systems, and the list goes on. What can keep you addicted? *Denial* denying there is a problem, or that you could be addicted; if those who love you are telling you they think you are addicted to something, do not let denial stop you from hearing them, or stop you from overcoming the problem and getting on with life.

The problem with living in denial is that everyone **but** you can tell what is going on, even young children, although they might not always know how to verbalize what they are seeing.

Some substances are going to require rehabilitation help to recover; telling yourself "I can do this on my own" will keep you locked into the addictive cycle and the misery will continue. BE WISE ENOUGH TO WANT A BETTER LIFE AND GET HELP! All addictions stem from anxiety, that is why when you conquer one addiction, another can and often does take its place. Seek help for dealing with anxiety. See Chapter A—Anxiety.

AFFAIRS: There is so much pain and tangled webs woven through affairs, the best rule of thumb is: Don't do it. Often those whose spouses or significant others have cheated on them, cheat themselves to "get even" and wind up hurting themselves and others. Partners, who have been cheated on, may not always realize consciously, that they are "getting even". The test would probably be, during the 1st encounter, did you even like, the person you wound up cheating with? There must be loyalty if a family is to feel secure in love and survive. In the case of a cheating partner, if you have an affair, that won't right the wrong that's been done and will cause more drama.

So, what if you've already had an affair? I do not agree that its always best to "bare your soul" to your mate, this can wind up being used against you in an argument down the road. Hopefully, if you have had an affair, you are now resolved not to do it again. Do explore with a counselor, your reasons for getting involved, and what you have learned from it. There are so many lessons in life, one thing I know for sure is that when we *get* the lesson we are never challenged with it again. If we do not get it, the faces and names change, but the lesson presents itself again and again.

While there are many reasons for affairs, boredom with one's life is probably the worst and one should explore why they are bored with life and living. If you feel guilt and sorrow, do work on self forgiveness as often as necessary.

If your partner has an affair, there will be much work to be done to repair trust. Whether to stay in the marriage or relationship is a matter of personal choice. Some high profile women stay, some leave but no matter what your choice, there is work to be done. Leaving a relationship doesn't mean that it is mentally *over*, you might find yourself questioning the whole thing for many years to come. I have seen instances where a wife will divorce her husband and then get back in the relationship anyway, it is my personal opinion that one should kick them out if you must, but don't get the divorce unless you are ABSOLUTELY sure it is over, and that is something you may not know for months. If you do leave and feel that it is completely over, leaving will not erase the pain, although it can ease it. If you do not work on forgiveness, you will carry mistrust into the next relationship, and cause that person to pay for something they did not do to you. See Chapters F—Forgiveness, G—Guilt.

AFFIRMATIONS: Many of us have been taught or learned from our care-givers to be expert in negative, self-talk. Those negative tapes can be changed, through disciplined, conscious, effort. Affirmations (praise, blessings) gets the joy moving, in your heart and in your life. "The true nature of man and woman is joy". Life's greatest lesson is said to be Love, and Joy is Love's partner.

Affirming the good in every situation, awakens joy in our hearts and lives. Fear of life, or situations, gives us more to fear about or stress over. Any good that could come in is blocked; remove the block and get good energy flowing in your life :-) Don't let delays stop your praise! Here is a list of my favorite affirmations, feel free to learn and use them. After a while, sit down and write out some of your own. You will find, as you go about your day, an affirmation will come up to fit most any situation.

AFFIRMATIONS FOR LIFE:

I AM CALM
I AM PURE SPIRIT
I AM PURE SPIRIT AND SPIRIT CAN FEEL NO PAIN
I AM A SPIRITUAL BEING HAVING A HUMAN EXPERIENCE
I AM A WORTHWHILE, LOVING PERSON
I AM FRIENDLY AND OTHERS ARE FRIENDLY TO ME
I AM KIND
I AM LOVE
I AM PATIENT
I AM PEACE
I AM STRENGTH
I AM A RADIANT BEING OF LIGHT
MY LIFE AND AFFAIRS ARE IN DIVINE ORDER

AGING: From the moment we are born, we begin to age. Some years are less noticeable than others, and its not until age 25 that we begin to seriously consider the fact that we are aging. Most 25 year olds think they are now "old." That just isn't the truth we discover, after we live several more years. The sobering that we get at age 25, is the waking up we need to get on the right path.

According to Astrology, we do not become adults until we are between the ages of 28—31, and have a transit known as the First Saturn Return. It is the time when, according to Astrology we become adults; we lay down our childhood garments and childish ways of acting and reacting, and take on our adult cloaks.

It is said, "Life begins at 40." I believe that is true, but like everything else, we have to settle in and get used to it. Around age 42, one starts feeling younger; by 45, in many cases, you feel younger than you did at age 25. The ages between 42 and 45, bring an opportunity to finally heal inner child issues once and for all. The opportunity to step into a new phase of life will present itself beginning with the opportunity to conquer one's ego. The 40's is also the time when mid-life crises, and poor decisions are made. When you get over it, you will wonder what hit you and how you could have made that decision in the first place. Instead of beating yourself up, forgive yourself and move on. Another lesson learned and a new chapter will begin.

The 50's, (which sounds ancient if you are under 35) is a glorious decade. So much depends upon attitude, but one does get many opportunities to "put on a new attitude." If you haven't been taking good care of yourself, you can find health issues cropping up; 50 is a great time to decide to embark on a fitness regime. Most 50 year olds are very proud to have lived to be a half a century, its great when you look and feel good.

If you absolutely and intensely dislike the winkles that are starting to show, then if your insurance won't cover, start saving for some cosmetic surgery. A reputable plastic surgeon can make them go away. If you hate that gray, it doesn't have to be a must that you wear it, coloring the hair can make you feel (and look) a lot better!

You might feel that its too late to exercise, but it's never too late to start and you will be very surprised at how fast the body responds.

We are never too old to change or learn new things, whether 60, 70, 80 or beyond, as long as we are healthy. Don't be afraid to learn, grow and be proud of what you have already accomplished. Just the fact that you have lived long enough to be a Senior Citizen is a HUGE accomplishment.

Aging brings "Rites of Passage", some we welcome, some we love, some we would rather do without; the more we welcome each chapter of our lives, the more peace and joy we will experience. If we live in the past, we will not know the joy of the present, nor will we motivated to set goals that will bring future joy.

It isn't a given that "with age comes wisdom", but if you pray or ask for wisdom, it will come, bringing with it the most awesome of growth. I am fond of saying: "I asked for wisdom, boy did I get it"!

AMBITION: If you have no ambition in your life, you will certainly meet up with depression at some point. Depression is the thief of ambition. No matter how tough you feel life is or how sad it might make you feel at times, your life has a purpose and meaning far greater than we realize until midlife.

Become friends with setting goals; without a goal we have no sense of direction. When you achieve one goal, give it some thought, and replace it with a new one. If a goal is set, and for one reason or another cannot be reached, don't beat yourself up or give up on ambition, set a new goal and go for it! Get excited about your life, ambition will be born. See Chapter A—Achieving Goals.

ANCESTORS: For a variety of reasons we may not have a very reliable record of our ancestors, or be able to go back past the great-grandparents unless someone in the family hands down good records or we consult a genealogist; we can also research for ourselves on the web, genealogy is a great hobby.

Nonetheless we are a product of the Ancestors who lived before us. Native Americans and other cultures have a very good grasp of the importance of Ancestors to the life. You might find it very rewarding and fun to know the family history you were born into. Each person is a beautiful thread in the rich tapestry of life woven by the ancestors who walked before them.

If we don't know their names, or anything about them we can still honor their Spirit and the Spirit within us by honoring ourselves and keeping good records for those born after us in the family. Its a good idea to keep records in more than one place, such as a personal safe and a safety deposit box, since we can not be sure we won't meet with a natural disaster at some point; keep your records as safe as possible.

ANGELS: Catholics and some other religions believe in Angels, other religions and beliefs call them "Guides." It is my belief that we all have a Guardian Angel (or main Guide) assigned to us at birth, who steps in whenever there is danger or a need; there are also legions of other Angel "helpers", or

Guides waiting to be called upon for assistance since they may not interfere, unless we ask.

Inviting Angels into your life or situation is a very easy thing to do. This can be done out loud or silently by asking: "Angels in charge of ______(Employment, Healing, Love, Relationships, tests or any other need) be here with me (us) now! Always remember to thank the Angels when you have seen them work in your life. Angels are Joyful Beings, where they are invited in, there is JOY. The natural state of man or woman is joy (somehow we got off the track on that, but the good news is that we can get back on track anytime we choose). We just have to make up our minds to do it.

As a young child in parochial school, I learned the following prayer:

ANGEL OF GOD,MY GUARDIAN DEAR,
TO WHOM HIS LOVE COMMITS ME HERE.
EVER THIS DAY BE AT MY SIDE
TO LIGHT AND GUARD,
TO RULE AND GUIDE.

I began a personal relationship with Angels when I was about 28. Through the years I have seen many dramatic happenings that only Angels could have answered to my calls.

One of the most dramatic was in the 80's; a car had been sitting in front of our house all day. We didn't have a very large front yard, so the street was pretty close to the large picture window in the living room of our home. That was the reason the car was so noticeable as it sat outside of our house. That evening around 7:00 p.m., a rather noisy car pulled up alongside the parked car. That got my attention, as I watched, a fire bomb was lit and thrown into the car. I had been on the phone with my friend, Dinah, and started yelling for my children to leave the room, I then told her what was going on. She said: "We are calling on the Angels right now to put out this fire" I said: "Amen" and got off the phone to call the fire department, by the time they got there, they said, "You were lucky, the fire put itself out." They advised me to call the police who had the car towed away.

After all the excitement was over, I called Dinah back, and we both said, "wow" to the experience. She also said, that wasn't "luck" that was the Angels at work. We knew the Angels had responded right away. They will do that for you, learn to call on them. Do Not forget to say Thank You!

ANGER: Anger is one letter away from **D**anger, I was amazed when I saw that pointed out! There are many causes of inner anger and rage. Some of us are born into dysfunctional families who don't know how to treat each other or anyone else. That can be handed down from generation to generation. You cannot teach another what you did not learn. Angry parents will raise angry children.

For others, a series of life events or losses can cause anger to start building up. Feelings of unfairness, perhaps anger at the self. Self directed anger has many causes, mistakes made, things one did or didn't do, dwelling on what you feel is wrong with your body or other things about yourself that you don't like. I have come to learn that mistakes are part of learning lessons. Life is a classroom for the soul; it is also my belief that certain lessons are part of our soul contracts and we are charged with the mission to overcome our less than desirable traits or ways we don't want to be so that we can become a good Role Model for others.

The important question is: do you control your anger, or, does it control you? If you know you have a temper, take steps to control it. Seek out an anger management course. Uncontrollable anger is destructive to one's own health and that of the health and well being of those around you.

Anger is a valid human emotion, sometimes without anger we would not change anything. If taught early on how to control it, it will not become a problem later on. If one has abusive parents or other caretakers, the battle with anger can be a lifelong challenge, until forgiveness work is done and a firm commitment made to change from an angry person to one who finds the joy from within.

Anger and substance abuse is a cocktail for disaster. Native Americans didn't call alcohol "fire water" for nothing.

If one is born into a family where alcohol or other drug use was acceptable, chances are they will be challenged by substance abuse in their own life. It took me many years to learn that alcohol, although legal, is a poison to the mind, body and spirit, and seems to bring anger to the surface more readily than if a person does not drink.

If you take a look within and find that you have too much anger, get yourself in for some anger management training if you can't find that in your city, get in for counseling pronto before anger causes you to get in trouble or drive away people you love. There is not too many good things that can be said for an angry person. See Chapter F—Forgiveness.

APOLOGIZE: We all make mistakes, some we never apologize for; doing something nice for someone after you know you have hurt them, does not *make up* for what was done. Three little words, "I am sorry", will go a long way towards healing any wounds. What if you have been hurt and never received an apology? It is a good idea to mentally affirm: "I fully and freely forgive you, I loose you and let you go on your way to your highest good as I go on to mine." Understand that others, even if they have hurt you, could be doing the best they could under the circumstances; if they knew better they would do better. If you walked in their shoes, experienced their life with all its joys and sorrows, you might find that you would react the same way.

What if you really know you should apologize, but cannot seem to say it? I wonder if that is because you feel that somehow you were *right*? The very least you can do to would be to send a card that says: I am sorry if I hurt or offended you, please accept my apology. I read this quote, but do not remember who said it: "People will not remember what you do, but they will remember what you say."

Parents should not be afraid to apologize to their children; children are very forgiving of parental mistakes and that teaches them early on how to apologize. Apologizing to your children will teach them that its the right thing to do for others. See Chapter F—Forgiveness.

APPLE: The old saying: "an apple a day, can keep the doctor away", is a good rule of thumb. Health is one of your most important commodities. What we put into our bodies determines what we get back in terms of body performance and well being. The time to take responsibility for your health is when you are well; it takes too long once illness happens to get back on our feet. Apples are one of the fruits that doctors feel will prevent cancer, (an antioxidant) especially the skins. Apple juice is very soothing after some surgeries. See Chapter N—Nutrition.

ANXIETY: Anxiety: From the dictionary: Main Entry: anx·i·ety Function: noun Inflected Form(s): plural -eties Etymology: Latin anxietas, from anxius Date: circa 15251 **a:** painful or apprehensive uneasiness of mind usually over an impending or anticipated ill **b:** fearful concern or interest **c:** a cause of anxiety**2:** an abnormal and overwhelming sense of apprehension and fear often marked by physiological signs (as sweating, tension, and increased pulse), by doubt concerning the reality and nature of the threat, and by self-doubt about one's capacity to cope with it. Miriam Webster Online Dictionary.

Even in the most natural forms of childbirth I believe we are born with anxiety. Not all that long ago, most babies were slapped on the rear within seconds after birth, to start the baby crying and get them going. The harder the birth experience, the more anxious the newborn will be, and in some cases traumatized. Childbirth today is often more gentle in terms of how the newborns are handled right after birth.

The level of anxiety we develop depends upon several factors, the emotional makeup of the family or care-givers, the society we live in, and our own soul contracts.

In every life some anxious times will appear. Anxiety is a very real feeling that affects all humans (and animals). To be over anxious and fearful however, leads to very unhappy, nervous living. If you have anxiety attacks, please seek professional help. We must also take some responsibility for overcoming anxiety. Wear either a clear quartz or rose quartz Crystal. Both have been known to help or alleviate anxiety. Rose Quartz Crystals are said to "heal the heart". See Chapter C—Crystals.

If medication is prescribed for anxiety, request a referral for therapy too, healing anxiety is not done by a pill alone but counseling or group therapy will help greatly.

Acupuncture, Chiropractic treatments, and/or a Reiki healing treatment by a local practitioner is also helpful. I have recently discovered a healing modality known as EFT, Emotional Freedom Techniques that is said to be very beneficial in relieving anxiety.

I have also read and believe: The more disconnected we feel from our *source*, or Creator, the more anxiety we will feel. Once I got it out of my *head* (intellect) and into my heart, that I am a Spiritual Being having a Human experience, I began to look at life as more of an adventure. It has been said: "Life is a journey to be savored, not a race, to be won."

ASTROLOGY: In the Zodiac there are 12 Astrological Signs, the Sun travels through the Signs much the same way we follow the yearly calendar. Signs change on approximately the 21st of each month. Every human being (whether they believe in Astrology or not) has a designated "Sun Sign" according to their date of birth.

The Sun Signs are:

Aries	Mar 21	to	April 21
Taurus	April 21	to	May 21
Gemini	May 21	to	June 21
Cancer	June 21	to	July 21
Leo	July 21	to	Aug 21
Virgo	Aug 21	to	Sept 21
Libra	Sept 21	to	Oct 21
Scorpio	Oct 21	to	Nov 21
Sagittarius	Nov 21	to	Dec 21
Capricorn	Dec 21	to	Jan 21
Aquarius	Jan 21	to	Feb 21
Pisces	Feb 21	to	Mar 21

These are approximate dates, if you are born close to the 21st of the month, consult a Professional Astrologer to find out exactly what sign you are born under. You might learn that you are "born on the cusp of two signs" which can explain why either sign (or both) seems to fit you better. There are many great books on the market on how the signs interact with each other; a good working knowledge of that is very helpful when meeting people for the first time.

Astrology is the set of instructions or blueprint of the life, we didn't know we are born with. Astrology can help you to understand yourself, loved ones, and people you just met. A Natal Birth Chart is a 360 degree circle, it looks like a pie cut into 12 slices. Each area, known as a "House" to Astrologer, denotes a certain area of one's life. Yes! You guessed it! Each House is ruled by one of the twelve Sun Signs.

A Natal Birth Chart is as unique to you, as your fingerprints. A Birth Chart is also called, The Natal Horoscope. You might hear a chart called a "Wheel" or simply, a Chart. They are one and the same. The chart is calculated from TIME, place and date of birth. It is so exact, even identical twins, born six minutes apart, at the same place, on the same date will have slightly different (but important) placements in the Natal Chart.

If the birth time is unknown, there are two methods available to Astrologers. A Solar Chart, while it will not give as much information, gives a very good interpretation as a Natal Chart. There is also a process called Rectification of the Natal Chart that will give a very accurate chart. Consult an Astrologer even if you don't know your birth time.

Astrology of youth can help you to understand your children in ways that aren't always possible in day to day living with children. An understanding of your own Natal Birth Chart is a great tool to understanding yourself; seek a qualified Astrologer for help in getting an understanding where the Planets were on the day you were born and what the promise is for your life.

Relationship charts, whether family, friends or other loved ones tell an interesting story of compatibility and will point out the areas that could be troubling in a relationship. It is a great idea to get that information **before** you fall in love.

ATTITUDE: "Change your Attitude, **Change** your life," is the truth. If you always do things the way you have always done them, you can ALWAYS expect to get the same results. Your Attitude is one thing totally under your care and control; at times, it will seem that it is the only thing we do have control of.

Temper tantrums are not cute even in young children. Become aware of the things you say, is it often something negative? How often do you go out of your way to be pleasant when you don't *have* to because of work or in other social situations? Has anyone, or several people told you that you need an *attitude adjustment*? If so, take heed. Get a small notebook, or just a small sheet of paper carried in your pocket will do. When you catch yourself or become aware that something you are about to say will be negative, or will put down someone else, make a little tally mark on the sheet, at the end of the day, total up the marks you have there, you might be quite surprised. Learn to bite your tongue. It is up to each individual to be a role model, and commit to being the best they can be, not the worst.

Do you often find yourself wanting some good experience in your life, then quickly saying "I know it won't happen anyway"? If so, do a cancel, cancel on that. Your good can't come to you if you believe it won't.

Attitude determines Altitude! Strive to see the good in every situation! I once heard a quote, author unknown: **"People will not remember what you do, but they will remember what you say."** Physical bruises go away and you can never seem to recall exactly how they looked, but you will remember often exactly what has been said to you. See Chapter N—Nagging.

AURA: We are so much more than our physical bodies! Everything in the Universe has an energy vibration that includes our thoughts, which are also a vibration. Many psychically in tune people can see the aura around others, animals, plants or trees. We can train ourselves to see the aura, it is an energy field and extends out from our body; the easiest place to actually see an aura is around the head and shoulders.

The Aura contains information corresponding to our emotions and state of health or disease. It will change colors according to our energy at any given time. Auras of objects such as stones, or crystals are essentially fixed. There are many great books and web sites having to do with the Aura, don't be afraid to explore! A shower is good not only to clean the body, but the Aura too, especially after a long or stressful day.

CHAPTER B

Babies, **B**ach Flower Remedies, **B**anish, **B**eauty, **B**ible, **B**irthday, **B**itterness, **B**lame, **B**lessing, **B**ody, **B**reaking up, **B**roken Heart

BABIES: Babies are wonderful, but remember they have real needs and require a lot of work. Be responsible about having them, and wait until you are ready. Babies are not the dolls little girls love to play with. There's nothing cute about colic and dirty diapers.

Babies will bring real change and challenge into your life experience. I do believe however, that parenting is life's most important job, and the richest of spiritual blessings, not to mention, a lot of FUN. Children make the holidays and general life worthwhile, especially when you look at life through the eyes of a child, full of wonderment. Besides that, clean babies smell wonderful!

Motherhood is forever. If we have great mothers or not so great mothers, we remember them forever. We grow up with our children and have to commit to being a good role model for them. Children learn by what we do, not by what we say for them to do. I have also learned that when your children are young, they bring you their toys, but when they are older, they bring you their babies.

If you are unhappy in your own life, having a baby will NOT *fix* anything! A child cannot and will not fix a bad relationship, marriage, or a lonely life. True, you won't be alone, but remember, you'll have to get up and fix breakfast or dinner, no matter what else is going on in your life. You will also have to support the children you bring into the world; the world expects you to, and you owe it to your children to take good care of them.

Having his baby does not guarantee that the child's father will love and support you even though you have his child. Many fathers are good dads, but just as many will walk away from both of you. In some cases, you might decide that you don't want the child to be around the other parent.

If a man is abusing you, getting pregnant will not make him stop even though he might claim to love the idea of becoming a father. Should you have a baby by someone who is abusing you? Probably better to prevent getting pregnant for the simple fact that if he is abusing you, he is going to abuse the child too at some point.

If the relationship with the child's father was less than ideal, you must make a pact with yourself not to take it out on the child. That can be a challenge especially if the child resembles the less than ideal partner you are no longer with, or the man you have come to hate or intensely dislike.

I believe that when a child comes into our life, it is at the time we need the most love. They love us unconditionally and if we love them back and do our best to raise them, that love is forever!

A note of caution: We cannot teach what we do not have! If your own self-esteem is not good, you will not be able to raise a child with good self esteem, UNLESS you put forth the time and effort to diligently work on your self esteem issues.

You are never sure of how good a job you've done, until they grow up. That doesn't mean feel guilty if they make the wrong choices for themselves. Children have their own learning experience, as we all do. The teenage years don't count in that measure, since they are still finding themselves and it is up to us to guide them to be their best. Too much freedom too early will not help them and can hurt them terribly. See Chapters P—Parenting, Post Partem Depression, S — Self Esteem, Single Parenting.

BACH FLOWER REMEDIES: Also called Flower

Remedies (found at a good local health food store or online) are known as "treatments for the soul" as opposed to medicines we take for our physical body. I prefer the Bach brand over others available. It's a matter of personal choice. A very important remedy is one by Bach Flower Remedies, "Rescue." This particular remedy comes not only in drops but in a cream too. Rescue can help you pull it together, when all the chips seem down. Study and learn about these important remedies, you will be glad you did. If a person is very ill, a few drops of Rescue on the wrist is very beneficial. This remedy has been said to save lives in the case of a person having a heart attack and does seem to help calm the Spirit.

BANISH: There are times in our lives, where we have to go beyond *letting go* and banish someone or something from our lives. We found they are not good for us, or to us, in one way or another. I like the French phrase for this, "I bid you Adieu." We might find ourselves doing this with family, including our children, friends, mates, partners, or acquaintances. Will we miss them? Yes! If the relationship is toxic it is the best thing to do. Once you decide to let go, let it be a clean break. Don't answer email, take calls or call them. If they have been in any way violent towards you, do not hesitate to get a restraining order from the courts.

Please note: I do not mean banish someone for whom you have a responsibility to as a means to shirk that responsibility. You have to look at each relationship and ask yourself, "did I do my best"? If you can honestly answer yes to that question, and you know in your heart they did not bring out the best in you then it is the right decision for the right reason.

Be aware that we do all change and sometimes we outgrow each other. Someone that brought out the best in you ten years ago, might not be bringing out the best in you now. I have known too many young girls who became pregnant and whose family kicked them out. Such action is not my idea of "banishment". Often, but not always, young girls would not become pregnant if the family openly and honestly talked about sex or if they felt loved and secure at home. See Chapter D—Dysfunctional.

Sometimes, we must banish certain attitudes, bad habits or ways of thinking from our life experience. If you are in the habit of beating yourself up emotionally, banish the thought; i.e., I am so stupid! If you catch yourself saying that, or any other negative thought towards yourself, do a "cancel, cancel" mental note and supply another affirming thought, such as "I am Pure Spirit and Spirit is well!".

If you are addicted to a substance or any of the number of things we can get addicted to, banish it from your life. Change your attitude, Changing your life pattern is something I believe in strongly and I believe anyone can change anything they choose to change regardless of age. The old saying "you can't teach an old dog new tricks" is just not true! We all have the ability to grow. All we have to do is get ready! For some of us, we have to get sick and tired of being sick, and tired.

The best way to figure out what needs to be changed is to make a list of things you like about your attitude and things you want to change. You might ask friends and family what they would like to see changed in your attitude. Don't allow it to hurt your feelings if they answer honestly (smile), just make the list and be open-minded to see the things that you might have to work on.

If you want to stop smoking, banish cigarettes from your life and home; banish junk food and choose to eat only healthy things for your body; banish some words from your vocabulary, such as cursing or even a mild, "I am so broke" when money seems scarce. "Broke" means that it cannot be fixed, and that is not the truth about your finances. Get your "banish" list together, (bid the things or attitudes you need to change adieu) starting from the top eliminate one bad habit at a time; by the end of this year, you will be a "New Person" and a happier one who can be proud of keeping a resolution or achieving a goal! See also Chapters A—Achieving Goals, Addiction, L—Letting go."

BEAUTY: Beauty does come from the inside out, if you are unhappy, no matter how pretty you are, you will not shine.

All the make up in the world will not help you. Try to get enough rest, as that is the time our body gets a chance to repair itself.

What if you have been told all your life that you are not pretty, or what if, no matter how often others tell you how pretty you are, you do not feel it? That is a strong indication that your self-esteem needs some work, PRONTO! You are worth committing to 90 days of conscious self-esteem work, you will change your life and how you look at yourself forever. See Chapter S—Self Esteem.

BIBLE:
Basic
Instruction
Before
Leaving
Earth

I believe that everyone should have a good working knowledge of this all time best selling book! Granted it is difficult to understand but there are many bible studies around; it is good for us to learn as much as we can; the more sacred books we take the time to get a basic understanding of, the better. There are times when the longing of the human heart and spirit can only find comfort and relief in Spirituality.

BITTERNESS: This is hatred's relative, where there is hatred, there will be bitterness, where there is bitterness, unhappiness resides. Sometimes bitterness can lead one into a victim role. A rut is so easy to get into, and so insidious or sneaky that we might not even recognize it. If we get stuck there, we can spend a great portion of our lives in that role. What a major waste of time, to live a life stuck in the bitterness of "if **only**, I would've, should've, could've." In life bad things happen to good people, things happen to every one of us, and could leave us bitter or unhappy if we dwell on what is wrong instead of what is right. Many states of mind can cause dis-ease in our physical bodies, anger, bitterness and stress are some of the worst. Beauty does come from the inside out and flows out to the world from within us.

If you are feeling especially down about life and the people in it, stop right then and there and take a few seconds to write down **five things** you are grateful for; it will immediately change your energy. It follows the premise that you cannot smile and frown at the same time. See Chapters A—Anger, F -Forgiveness, G—Gratitude, and S—Stress.

BIRTHDAY: The day you were born is a day to be celebrated, no matter how you feel about getting "older". The whole month holds what I call "birthday energy"; new growth, new ideas and new happiness will be found in the coming year, if you get excited about your life. Celebrate You! Many mother's do (and should) celebrate the "birth day", the day their children were born; it truly is an event that is not forgotten. Don't forget to buy yourself a birth day present each year, you have earned it!

In our life cycle, some years are by far better than others, your attitude about yourself is most important. If you aren't excited about your life, GET EXCITED, it is a matter of choice. See Chapter S—Self Esteem.

BLAME: It is easier to blame other people or circumstances when we are unhappy. It's important that we take responsibility for our actions, and responsibility for our choices and subsequent *messes*. A choice made in haste, can make one feel like years of their life went to *waste*. We all have lessons to learn on making right choices. "The devil made me do it" doesn't cut the mustard, we have free will.

Do we have temptation, oh my, certainly so, I'm not negating that. Once out of childhood, it is up to us to take responsibility for our actions and make up our own mind if something offered is good for us. See Chapter C—Choices

BLESSING: The art of Blessing others, is a unique way of spreading peace and joy to the world; almost magically, blessings come back to us. To bless ourselves, loved ones, and our world attunes us to the Divine.

Blessing makes things right and comfortable. It seems easy enough, but we have to remember to do it, and staying focused in the midst of a busy life is not always easy. Just do the best you can, after some time of conscious blessing, it will become an automatic habit that is not only good for you, but everything and everyone around you.

Bless everything and everyone, even those you do not particularly like or feel fear of, like a bumblebee. Blessing others puts a positive focus in one's mind, and when in a positive state, creative energy flows. It is a quick and easy way to raise your own energy when you feel out of sorts, or even if you don't, it will still raise your energy vibration.

A blessing can be as simple as "What a beautiful day." "I love your smile..." "My state of health is such a blessing." Attuning your thinking to the art of blessing will insure that you will feel good most of the time. If you find yourself unhappy much of the time, instead of looking at what is wrong in your life, learn to look at what is right and is a blessing to you, before you know it, you will be looking for the good all around you and find yourself more at peace. When we learn to bless others, blessings come back to us multiplied.

BODY: We get only one, and too many of us don't like the one we have or some of its parts. It becomes a real shock when one of the parts stop working or is injured, then we realize how much we have taken even simple things for granted. Children should be taught that their body is a temple. As adults, we can teach ourselves if we didn't get it from our childhood caretakers, that our body is a sacred temple.

If you look around, its easy to see many people who aren't taking care of themselves, their teeth, hair, skin, clothing, or in general, their lives. How many times have you been in a public restroom and watch others leave a stall without washing their hands?

In these days of quick showers, every one should take at least one real bath a week; there is a lot to be said for soaking in a tub of water. Not only is it very calming, but a good soak is great for the skin :-) When all else fails, let a bubble bath take you away!

If there is some part of your body that you absolutely would like to change, start a savings plan to help you get it fixed. What if you are injured? Remember that you are still you, and life can still be good. Things might have to change a bit to compensate, but that does not mean that you cannot live a full life no matter what the injury or handicap involved.

BREAKING UP: No matter how you slice it, or what you call it, breaking up is hard to do. We all have at least one person we keep tucked into a corner of our hearts as we move on in life. Often breaking up is harder because we don't like to admit we might have been wrong about someone, or they aren't the person we thought they were. It is no reflection on *poor judgment* when we find someone is not right for us. There are times when someone right for us now, may not be right for us ten years down the road. People do grow and change and if one partner does not accept growth and refuses to change, they just might turn out to not be right for us.

Breaking up is easier if we are the one requesting the break up; if not, we might feel rejected or abandoned. That is not the truth about you. Sometimes we can look back years later and see that it was the best thing that happened to us. An older lady told me once, "Don't worry, the right person can't come along if the wrong person is blocking the door." I found out that she was right! The Universe has a way of moving people or circumstances out of our life if it is not in our best interests or for our highest good to have them stay. See Chapters B—Banish, L—Letting Go.

BROKEN HEART: We hear the phrase suffering from a broken heart. Our hearts can and do certainly ache, but I tend to stay away from *broken* phraseology. My daughter informed me once when I said I was "broke." "Mom, don't say that, broke means it can't be fixed." One thing I know for sure is that our hearts are resilient and that is the good news. I am not invalidating feelings at all, that is not my intent, just suggesting that it isn't *broken* forever, although surely, it feels like a forever thing when our heart aches.

I often hear clients say: "I'll never be able to love someone like I loved him or her". I suggest that isn't the truth. In time, you will find you are able to love someone even more than the person you are breaking up with.

Moving on is sometimes a must, in spite of fairy tale "lived happily ever after" endings. The main question is how do we go about that, first we grieve, (letting it be okay for us to do so). There are 7 stages to grief. See Chapter G—Grief.

If there has been no closure to the break up, such as when a person just walks away, it is important that we give ourselves closure. The technique I have used, and taught to others, is to write a letter to the person, putting down all your feelings; I do not mail this to them (as it will not change things) instead, I burn this letter, with a short mantra:

LOVE MANTRA

for letting go
I BLESS YOU
I RELEASE YOU
I SET YOU FREE
I SET ME FREE
I LET YOU BE
I LET ME BE
(received in email, author unknown)

Years back, there was a song that began with, "Gonna wash that man right outta my hair," and I always used that as a place to start when I felt ready to move on. Either I did it myself or went in for a new *do*. Then I sat down and took an inventory of the relationship, what I felt were my strengths, and weaknesses, what if any mistakes I made. The reason I would put this down on paper, is that it worked for me, to be able to view objectively both sides of the list, self-improvement is a very good thing and what we strive for. The purpose of looking at our weaknesses is NOT to beat ourselves up for them, but to improve on what we don't care for. That is what growth is all about. Does a breakup mean that we weren't soul mates after all? No, not at all. I am not into the hype of today that says only one person is our soul mate. If that were true, there would surely be many unhappy people in the world who never got into another relationship or never married again.

What is true is that not all soulmate relationships feel great, nor do we stay forever with one person. Soulmate relationships are for the growth of both people involved, for our highest and best good, which doesn't always feel like a happy space, as we are moving towards our highest and best good.

Hearts do break, so be sure to treat those entrusted to your care gently. What helped me the most in affairs of the heart was to realize I am a Spiritual Being having a Human experience. Once I *got* that out of my head and into my heart, life felt more like an adventure and not so cut and dried. See also Chapter F—Forgiveness.

CHAPTER C

Career, Caring, Chakras, Chaos, Childbirth, Childhood, Chiropractor, Choices, Christianity, Cleaning, Closure, Commitment, Communicate, Comparing, Computers, Confusion, Control, Creativity, Creator, Crossroad, Crying, Crystals, Culture, Cursing.

CAREER: Beside time spent with family and friends, this is where you will spend the majority of your time. If you love what you do it will be easier on you; if not a great deal of energy will be drained from you just getting through the hours you need to put in at work.Unless one is born wealthy, we will either have to work or start our own business in order to support ourselves and a family. Should you decide to start your own business there is help available through the Small Business Administration and possibly other help available through your state, do a web search on your state, http://www.yourstate.gov/ and look under the business link, you will find a wealth of information on what is available.

We might find after years of schooling that we do not like or cannot find employment in the career we chose; or for one reason or another we get bored and want to change careers. There is nothing wrong with changing careers in fact many of us do so in our lifetime due to choice or companies downsizing or closing. The important thing is that we move forward without beating ourselves up or with regrets. If we really believe that we are Spiritual Beings having a Human Experience, life becomes more of an adventure as we move on. Don't be afraid to try something new! Don't be afraid to dust off a dream and make it happen for yourself!

CARING: To have a caring spirit is a great blessing, to some of us it comes easy others have to work on it. Some folks only care about themselves, and other folks have care confused with "control." To care about others is a very good quality and one the world needs more of in today's society.

I always cringe when I hear the words "I don't care," my thoughts are that we all must care about every aspect of our lives and our world if it is to be more comfortable, or a better place for everyone to be. Those that truly do not care about others just didn't get enough love as a child or were not taught to develop a caring heart. Caring is a learned response (although some people are born with this quality) and something we can change, if only we will take the time and be interested enough about life to do so.

CHAOS: Some lifestyles are chaotic. We choose whether to live in chaos or peace. We may have learned in a dysfunctional home how to be chaotic, but we can choose to stop the chaos in our lives. My Grandmother used to say, "Cleanliness is next to Godliness," there is a lot to be said for a clean, orderly home. If your home is disorganized, chances are your life will be too. Take an interest in all aspects of your life. Work on self esteem. See Chapter S—Self Esteem.

CHAKRAS: The word chakra is Sanskrit for 'wheel' or 'disk' and signifies one of seven basic energy centers in the body. Each of these centers relates to major nerves branching forth from the spinal column. There are 7 major Chakras, and many minor ones throughout our body.

Chakras also correlate to levels of consciousness, colors, sounds, body functions, and more. A very good website to learn about chakras and their energy is: http://www.myss.com/chakrasflash.asp

A friend sent me this via email. I believe this is an ancient tool for Protection and/or to Clear the Chakras:

I breathe in Light through the center of my heart,opening my heart into a beautiful ball of Light allowing myself to expand.

I breathe in Light through the center of my heart, allowing

the Light to expand; encompassing my throat chakra and my solar plexus chakra In one unified field of Light within, through, and around my body.

I breathe in Light through the center of my heart,allowing the Light to expand; encompassing my brow chakra and my navel chakra in one unified field of Light within, through, and around my body.

I breathe in Light through the center of my heart, allowing the Light to expand; encompassing my crown chakra and my base chakra in one unified field of Light within, through, and around my body.

I breathe in Light through the center of my heart, allowing the Light to expand; encompassing my alpha chakra and my Omega chakra in one unified field of Light within, through, and around my body. I allow the Wave of Melatron to move between these two points. I AM a unity of Light

I breathe in Light through the center of my heart, allowing the Light to expand; encompassing my eighth chakra and my upper thighs in one unified field of Light within, through and around my body. I allow my emotional body to merge with my physical body. I AM a unity of Light.

I breathe in Light through the center of my heart, allowing the Light to expand; encompassing my ninth chakra and my lower thighs in one unified field of Light within, through, and around my body. I allow my mental body to merge with my physical body. I AM a unity of Light.

I breathe in Light through the center of my heart, allowing the Light to expand; encompassing my tenth chakra and to my knees in one unified field of Light within, through, and around my body. I allow my spiritual body to merge with my physical body, forming the unified field. I AM a unity of Light.

I breathe in Light through the center of my heart, allowing the Light to expand; encompassing my eleventh chakra and my upper calves in one unified field of Light within, through, and around my body. I allow the Oversoul to merge with the unified field. I AM a unity of Light.

I breathe in Light through the center of my heart, allowing

the Light to expand; encompassing my twelfth chakra and my lower calves in one unified field of Light within, through, and around my body. I allow the Christ over soul to merge With the unified field. I AM a unity of Light.

I breathe in Light through the center of my heart, allowing the Light to expand; encompassing my thirteenth chakra and my feet in one unified field of Light within, through, and around my body. I AM unity of Light.

I breathe in Light through the center of my heart, allowing the Light to expand; encompassing my fourteen chakra and to below my feet in one unified field of Light within, through, and around my body. I allow the Source's Presence to move throughout the unified field. I AM a unity of Light.

I breathe in Light through the center of my heart, I ask that the highest level of my Spirit radiate forth from the center of my heart. I radiate forth throughout this day I AM a unity of Spirit.

Note: When this is said a couple of times a day for a while, you will only have to say: "Unity Chakra"...and the process will be done without the entire Invocation. (author/source unknown) I received this long ago in email from a friend. If anyone knows the author, please email me and let me know so that I might give proper credit to the author or source. I suspect this is an ancient tool for chakra clearing, and is much needed today. Get those wheels spinning in the right direction!

CHILDBIRTH: The entire process of childbirth from conception to delivery, can be easy or difficult, so much depends on what the Mother is going through while she is carrying her child. Even under the best of circumstances, it is an awesome but difficult time, as one adjusts to the hormonal and body changes. The ideal situation is to have support during the pregnancy from someone you love, who loves you in return. If you find yourself alone during this time, or emotionally isolated from those around you or scared, take extra care to do one nice thing for yourself everyday.

Nurse Midwives provide awesome personal care during the pregnancy and childbirth. If you are very unhappy during your pregnancy, please talk to your health care provider about what is going on. The happier you are, the calmer your baby will be.

It is my belief that God sends a child into a woman's life at the time She needs the most love. Take good care of yourself and your baby! Remember it can take your body 2 years to recover from childbirth.

If after delivery, you feel unusually sad, please talk to your care provider, post partem depression is a very real and treat-able condition. Most care providers recommend that you continue to take the pre-natal vitamins, listen to them, as the change after childbirth includes a huge drop in hormones. See also Chapter P—Post Partem Depression.

Not all childbirth experiences end happily with a healthy baby, no matter how good you tried to take care of yourself. I believe (after several miscarrages myself) that the little soul just was not ready to be born yet. I wrote this in honor of the children I didn't get to meet.

Little One I didn't get to know,
I am sad because you just had to go.
Back to the Heavens and the Angels care
We are tied together by love I do declare!
We will meet again in heaven one day
and have many chances to play.
Until then, when I look upon a Star
I'll remember the Baby Angel that you are!
Your place cannot be taken by another
and I will always be your Mother!
Be well little Baby Angel of mine
All of us will be okay in time!

CHILDHOOD: For many children, the world is a hard place to grow up in. They are the least equipped to defend themselves. If blessed to have a nurturing environment at home, school can be an absolute WAR ZONE. It is true that children are the meanest to other children.

Such abuse, name calling, etc., MUST BE STOPPED. The place to stop begins at home; **teach tolerance,** as soon as your toddler is getting around, and you will spread LOVE. Value the little ones today, they will become tomorrow's leaders or maybe tomorrow's criminals.

When children are treated harshly it changes who they will become. If they are never allowed to play and have fun, they will forget how to smile easily and as adults will not be able to relax. They grow quickly and when they are grown you begin to realize that you didn't have that much time with them after all.

Children will try our patience and can "get on our last nerve." It isn't until we are grandparents that we realize that much of what children do is merely "kid stuff," all children do it and usually at the same stages. If your children are getting on your nerves, talk to someone, find support either at church, or through therapy or parenting groups. Issues don't seem so bad when they are shared, and people are happy to help when they know we are attempting to do the right thing. See also Chapters A—Anger, P—Parenting, S—Single Parenting.

CHIROPRACTIC: "Chiropractic is a health care philosophy that believes the body has the ability to heal itself when given the chance through removal of nerve interference caused by vertebral subluxation. Chiropractic believes that the nervous system controls human anatomy and physiology and interference of this will place the body in a state of dis-ease.

Dis-ease is a term used by chiropractors to describe a lowered state of existence for the human body, which affords lowered resistance leading to symptoms. The 'vertebral subluxation complex' (VSC or subluxation) is the cornerstone of the art, philosophy and science of chiropractic.

Chiropractors utilize various examination procedures to analyze and detect the existence of subluxations in the patient's spine. These procedures may include palpation of the spine with the hand, range of motion examination, nerve reflex and muscle examination, postural and x-ray examination. Once the findings are reported to the patient the chiropractor will recommend a series of treatments which may include adjusting the spine to remove subluxation, modalities to help reduce pain and spasms and therapeutic exercises to help strengthen the spinal musculature and improve posture.

Chiropractic is a safe and effective form of healing without the use of drugs and surgery. Over 90% of the public that has utilized chiropractic reports being satisfied with the treatment they had received. And chiropractic is very safe with the risk of serious injury greater than 1 in 1 million" Dennis P. O'Hara D.C., to learn more please visit: http://www.chirosense.com/

I am sure that chiropractic saved my life. In the beginning I was as skeptical as the average person about chiropractic care. I have now been a patient of this remarkable health system for 30 years. It is so good to feel great!

CHOICES: The choices we make for ourselves from about age 12 on, are so important. If we learn to make good choices for ourselves the high school years will be happy. If we make poor choices while in high school, it can mess up our life and change it forever. So much during the teenage years depends upon how loved you are, the rest of our lives depends upon how much we love ourselves. The more we love ourselves, the better choices we will make. If you find that you don't love yourself enough, work on building self-esteem. It is important to think of what the consequences will be when making choices, as every action brings a reaction. We have FREE WILL and with that can choose to do the right or the wrong thing; we must remember that making the wrong choices for ourselves means we can spend the rest of our life living with the results.

Training yourself to make good choices is well worth the effort. Impulsive choices might not turn out to be a good thing. Think on what someone suggests and ask yourself "Is this the best thing for me?" or, "Is this for my highest and best good?" I am a Christian, and when I get an idea, a Minister taught me to ask: "Is this of God"? I was told that if I asked that, and if it wasn't of God then the idea of doing something or making a change would leave.

There are many excellent self-help books available on making good choices; the thing is, we have to want to. If we are prone to self destructive behavior (some of us realize this, some of us do not) get some counseling help in addition to the self help books. See also Chapters A—Anger, D- Denial, F—Forgiveness, S — Self Esteem.

CHRISTIANITY: I feel that living a Christian life is the best way for me. I am certain that I would not have come to this point in my life, without the many prayers I said daily. There have been published accounts of the importance of praying for someone who is ill. Its been proven that those in group one, who were prayed for, did better in handling, managing or healing their situation than those in group two who were not prayed for.

Not everyone is looking for the right spiritual path, nor are they aware they should be seeking it. I strongly believe that the world would be a better place if everyone found their perfect spiritual path! There is nothing wrong with studying various forms of religion to decide which is best for you. If you do choose a spiritual path, and build a strong faith, you will have better coping skills in life.

There are several TV Ministries that I love, **"The Hour of Power"** is one, with **Rev. Schuller**, I learned a lot from him, and hope to one day visit the Crystal Cathedral in CA. **Joyce Meyers** Ministry, **There is Life In The Word**, **Creflo Dollar**, **T.D.Jakes**, and the **Paula White** Ministry, are among my favorites. Find one that you resonant with and start learning. It is my opinion that more programming like **T.B.N** and less shoot'em, or blow'em up programs on in the home, would lead to less violence in the world.

My personal choice for a home Church is Unity. Unity Churches of Christianity are located throughout the Country and is my favorite place to refuel spiritually; find yours!

CLEANING: My Grandmother used to say "Cleanliness is close to Godliness", one thing I know for sure is that living in a clean environment gives you a sense of peace.

In these days of so many chemicals in our cleaning solutions, its best to use rubber gloves, they are no longer big and bulky; our skin is like a sponge and it soaks up whatever we put our hands into or whatever we put on our skin.

If you feel your life is out of control or you are just not happy with it, get busy and **clean up your act!**

CLOSURE: In the course of our life, there will be relationships, or chapters of our lives (as I call them) that just don't seem to end right; the other person didn't get a chance to say goodbye (death) or the other person wouldn't say goodbye (someone who walks out of your life, (I call that silent abuse).

If you have a relationship that seems to have no closure, it is a perfectly fine idea to do a little closure ceremony for yourself. Write a letter to that person, explaining just how you feel; how the abandonment hurt you and how you have not been dealing with it well; get all feelings written down that come to mind. Do not mail or give them the letter, (this is a gift to yourself, the closure is for you). Safely burn it; while it is burning, take some deep breathes; when you let the breathe go, let the pain you just wrote about go with it; do at least 10 of these cleansing breaths; once the letter is burned, do the forgiveness mantra. See Chapters A—Abuse, Forgiveness, L—Letting Go.

COMMITMENT: Women want it, men run from it (at least until they get ready to commit). A commitment doesn't mean we own another person lock, stock and barrel, but there are many people who feel that they actually do. The best gift you can give yourself and those you consider family, is a peaceful home life. WHO you commit to is of the utmost importance. It will determine how easy or challenging your future will be.

Choosing a partner because they are "cute or fine" or have

a great body, should never be your only criteria for what you want in a partner. Decide what inner qualities you would like in your partner and choose according to those. Don't let loneliness choose your partner for you! I recommend reading "Are You The One For Me", by Barbara DeAngeles, Ph.D.

Once you have made the choice in partners, give it your best shot. If you can answer the question: "Did you do your best" when it comes to anything in life, with a resounding "yes" even if it doesn't work out as expected, you can still be proud of yourself.

COMMUNICATE: The more comfortable you are with yourself and who you are, the better you will be able to communicate with others. We cannot count on another person to know what we need or want just because they know us well.The better we communicate with others the better our relationships will work. It's been said a woman will say "let's talk" and a man will freeze up, but good communication is what insures long lasting, happy relationships. If you feel shy or do not feel that you communicate well, get some help; either classes, self help books or therapy will teach you what you need to know to be a good communicator.

COMPARING: If you constantly compare yourself to others it will be very difficult to be who you are or to be happy with what you have. We live in a society that begins to compare us to others at birth, i.e., "average birth weight," and it goes on from there.

Sometimes, what other people own appears to be more or better, other times, it's "she or he looks so much better than me," "my nose is too big, eyes too small, etc., until we can hardly stand ourselves and our subconscious mind is commanded and trained to see only what is wrong, instead of seeing what is right. Get excited about your life and the things that are right in your world, if there are physcial things you

you do not like about yourself, find out what to do to change it. Remember, you are a child of a loving Creator and you deserve to be happy with your life! Your life is a gift, what you do with it is your gift back.

COMPUTERS: This is the age of technology and computers are an amazing source of information. The world is now at our fingertips. Anyone who isn't familiar with computers, get some computer classes or training from a friend or relative. It won't be long before the home computer is as important as the television set in the home.

Online safety and security is a must and just as important as offline safety. It is a good idea to teach your children that "stranger danger" applies to those they meet on computers as well as in everyday life. There are pedophiles out there who prey upon children so do pay attention to your children and teens online activity. For more information on protecting your children online visit: http://www.fbi.gov/publications/pguide/pguidee.htm

While it is realistic that two people can meet online and become very good friends it is probably unrealistic to fall in love with someone you have never met. So wait until you meet and spend time together is my rule of thumb. If you find yourself in a position of wanting to meet someone offline, make sure you meet in a public place the first time and that at least one friend or loved one knows who you are going to meet and where.

I have been privileged to meet many friends online and then in person, we must remember, that there are good people in the world but unfortunately, there is what is known as "stranger danger"!

CONFUSION: At various times in our life we will feel confusion; it may concern a person you met or know, a decision you have to make, or about what to do next. Does that mean you are a weak person? No! Confusion at times is just part of the Human Condition and we wonder "What shall I do?"

Learning to Ground and Center yourself will allow you to feel clearer. Sharing with a trusted friend, mentor or advisor is also a good thing, as long as you make up your own mind and do not wind up doing what someone else wants you to do. After all is said and done, you will be the one who has to live with it. A good Affirmation for this: I am pure Spirit and Spirit cannot be confused! See Chapter G—Grounding.

CONTROL: Our struggle for control begins around age two. (Although, any parent of a newborn would swear it begins with the newborn stage). Some folks never let go of attempting to control everyone and everything around them. It's a good idea to remember that there is a Higher Power in charge of running things, and has been doing a good job of it for millions of years.

If things have to be your way or no way at all, take a long hard look at that and try to remember that other people have to make up their own minds on certain things. No matter how much you love them, they are still individuals with their own soul contract and lessons to learn. At times, "bite your tongue" applies here. There are many great self help and motivational books out, find one that speaks to you, and begin to change yourself from controlling to allowing others to be who they are. The sun rises and the moon sets without any help from you and many other situations in your life that will work out quite well without you insisting they have to be your way.

If you attempt to control people in your life, please remember, control is a form of abuse. Their parents already raised them and there is no need for you to take up where they left off. We surely do teach and learn from each other throughout our entire lives, but that does not mean bending another person's will to suit you. Love and Guidance, are healthy ingredients in relationships, control is not!

Often you will hear a person say "I meant well". Control can be well meaning, or an indication you do not trust the other person not to screw things up, and feel you must take charge. Please remember their is a Higher Power in charge, one who has been doing a good job of it well before you were born. Kindly give your opinion on things brought to you by a friend or loved one, but do allow them to make up their own mind and detach yourself from the outcome. See Chapter D—Detachment.

CREATIVITY: Everyone is creative, tapping into creative energy is not only a release but can be very exciting and exhilarating! Begin with art projects, do not be afraid to explore where your creative energy lies. For some it is in art, writing, crafts, photography, acting or dance; find yours.

Creative energy does seem to come and go. The more stressed or unable to relax we are, the less creative energy we have. The more we work on raising our energy vibration, not only will we feel better, but the light gets creative energy flowing. Learn as much as you can about becoming a Light-worker. You will be amazed at how your life will change. See also Chapter G—Grounding.

CREATOR: Finding the connection and resonating your spirit with that of the Great Spirit, Higher Power, Allah, God, Creator, Goddess, (whatever name you call your Spiritual Deity), will give you a sense of connection to your source.

No matter what we choose to believe, we must allow for differences in opinion and treat other's opinions with respect. I believe that our souls are charged with the mission to find and walk a Spiritual Path as we live our lives and be a good role model for others. Does a belief in reincarnation mean that one does not believe in God? Many people I know who are open to the possibility of reincarnation have a strong belief in one Creator

I read or heard somewhere "much of the disconnection and discontent human beings feel is due to not being connected with their Spiritual Source". I agree with that statement. We need a sense of purpose in our lives. There will be times when you will be alone in this world, no matter how many people you know; if you are connected to God (or whatever name you prefer for the Diety you serve) you are never alone! See Chapters P—Prayers of Protection, R—Reincarnation.

CROSSROAD: "Tis easy enough to be pleasant, when life flows like a song. But the man worthwhile is the one who will smile when everything goes dead wrong." Ella Wheeler Wilcox

No matter how stable we have set our lives to be, the one constant in this world is that everything will change. Children grow up, marriages fail, partners die, jobs change or we find ourselves in the midst of a natural disaster; no matter what causes the change, we will be at a crossroad in life needing to chose what to do next. Those are the times when we'll ask ourselves or others "what should I do?" and feel like the answer alludes us. Since I am a Psychic Reader, I do believe that its quite okay to get an opinion from an objective party that you trust, whether that be a loved one, pastor or a reader; remember that no matter what the suggestion, the choice is always up to you and you have to live with it. Our Faith is a great help when making life altering decisions. If you are in the midst of grieving for a loved one, try to wait at least six months before making any drastic changes.

If you are know within your heart that you are feeling hurt, angry, lonely or tired (HALT) and need to make a life decision, don't be afraid to seek out professional help; it doesn't indicate that you are crazy, it means you are human and need a bit of help making a decision on where to go from here. What if you have no insurance, and cannot afford professional help? There are many great self help books available, find one that speaks to your heart when you pick it up. Find resources in the City you live in, many have low cost or free services for those who need them.

There are times we make decisions to improve our life better, and we are surprised to find out that we are grieving what we left, especially if we are unsure of what is next; that is perfectly normal and its important that we allow ourselves to grieve. I have often heard the saying "When a door closes, a window always opens"; I don't care much for that, I think it should be "When one door closes another door always opens". As long as we are breathing and of sound mind, opportunity will present itself. See Chapters B—Banish, G—Grief.

CRYSTALS: There are many crystals available to us besides the most familiar quartz crystal. Crystals resurfaced in the late 1980's but are not to be considered "New Age" only; evidence of crystals dates back to ancient Africa, Egypt, Mexico, Russia and Native American Cultures. A crystal is a stone whose energy resonates with ours inwardly. Crystal vibrations have been known to calm and are believed to heal.

I personally experienced such a healing 15 years ago when

I began to have the type of anxiety attacks that felt just like a heart attack. An older friend told me to wear a clear quartz crystal and the anxiety attacks would go away. I thought that to be a little strange, but decided to give it a go after leaving yet another emergency room, where I felt scorned (once the heart tests were over) by the nurses since I was "only" having an anxiety attack. I found a small, clear quartz crystal, bought a little bag to place it in, and carried it tucked inside my bra. The anxiety attacks left and I have not been troubled by them since UNLESS I do not wear the crystals for some time. I have since added several other small crystals to what I now call, my "Medicine Bag". There are many good sites that can be found by doing a web search on Crystals.

CULTURE: We are all born in one culture or another. Accepting others, no matter what their culture is a good quality to cultivate. Respecting our differences, and being friendly is such a kind way to live! There really is not one superior culture over another. It is appalling to see or hear minority or other races downgrade another minority, yet they do. Prejudice is an insidious and hurtful thing, if the world is to be a better place for all, ALL must learn to live together in harmony. Live and let live is a good rule of thumb. See Chapter P—Prejudice.

CURSING: Children learn to cuss in the home, or from other adult relatives and their peers; toddlers might learn to curse before they can say the alphabet, teenagers think its a "cool" thing to do and adults seem to like the shock value and think their cursing drives their point home. I have witnessed people from other countries learning curse words before they learn good language skills. Interestingly enough, the people with "potty mouths" usually have rotten teeth. If a person cares little about their human brothers and sisters, uses unkind language when upset with family or friends, chances are they do not care about themselves; although I have heard very well groomed, professional people cuss like "drunken sailors".

In our society, there is too much cursing going on. Even a *little* word like d—n, carries a powerful punch for discordant energy to abound even though it has only 4 little letters. If you think about it, when using the D word,, what are you asking for?

There are many who put the name God before it; now they are asking for the Creator to "God d—n" **everything**, Is it any wonder the world is in so much turmoil and pain?

Once many years ago, I was sitting on a bed, with my head in my hands, wondering why my life was such a mess. I heard in my head the question, "Why do you curse so much, you are getting what you asked for! It dawned on me then, that I learned to curse from family and peers, so came by it naturally, BUT I was harming my own life and myself. I have since learned how to bless! See Chapters B—Blessing, M—Mouth, T—Tolerance.

CHAPTER D

Dating Pt I, Dating Pt II, Death, Decades, Denial, Depression, Detachment, Divine Order, Divine Self, Divorce, Dress, Drugs, Dying, Dysfunction.

DATING Part I: I often hear: "I dislike the dating game", that always makes me want to scratch my head, since I don't know any other way to wind up in a committed relationship, but to date. Dating is a good thing and allows us to get to know another person and decide if we really like spending time with them or not. A test of that would be, when you are with this other person, do you feel your best, or do they bring out the worst in you? Are you dating to get out with someone, get to know them and have a good time, or do you have an agenda? The agenda of course would be, asking, is this "the one"? Give yourself the chance to get to know someone before asking yourself that question. Too often, we take more care choosing our clothing than we do relationships; give yourself time to get to know a person.

There are many great dating services available now. If you feel that you aren't getting out enough, search out one in your area and meet other like-minded people. There is no age limit on dating, go and have a good time. Most cities have singles clubs, so do some churches. Find one that offers activities you like or are interested in. You may not meet anyone to date, but you just might have a great time, and meet like-minded friends. My Grandmother used to say "You will kiss a lot of frogs before the prince comes along." I never understood that when I was younger, but I found out it is true.

Men these days don't call themselves "dogs" for nothing, there are plenty of dogs out there, some are poodles, some pit bulls but many of them will play the same game, chase until they conquer and then run off. I highly recommend a book entitled "Are You The One For Me" by Barbara De Angelis, Ph.D, which gives a list of good questions to ask when you meet someone.

Today, we have computers and that has opened the possibility of meeting someone online anywhere in the world! While it is realistic that two people can meet online and become very good friends it is probably unrealistic to fall in love with someone you have never met. So wait until you meet and spend time together is my rule of thumb. If you find yourself in a position of wanting to meet someone offline, make sure you meet in a public place the first time and that at least one friend or loved one knows who you are going. We do have to be cautious, while at the same time remembering that there are good people in the world; just get to know them well before you give your heart and sometimes your power away.

DATING- Part II: Biracial/Bicultural/Interfaith Dating. Millions of biracial children have been born to testify to the fact that we can, "Love One Another." Love knows no color. Although some folks think so, there is no "perfect" race; all humans bleed red blood. There is no truth to the thinking that one minority is not just as good as any other. Mean, prejudice, and small-minded people perpetrate that thinking. It is a fact that most of us were taught by family what to think or feel towards another race.

There is no baby born prejudiced. It is a learned response. If you find yourself being asked out by someone of a different race or culture, it's a good idea to think ahead of time about how your family is going to feel. You can find yourself "between two worlds," not accepted in either. People might, gawk, stare, or look at you with hate in their eyes, so do be prepared. If you are a person who really cares *what other people think* this could be quite painful for you in the long term. If you think it is only your race that is prejudiced, think again, that is not so. Many races seem to think theirs is the best.

Interfaith dating can present hurdles later for the couple and families involved. It doesn't have to as long as each person commits to respecting the religious beliefs of the partner. How committed you are to each other will be a strong fortress against the beliefs of other family members.

All of this should be discussed between the couple early on and a good rule of thumb is to pay attention to how the person you are dating feels about your race, culture, or religion as a whole. That attitude might determine what you will hear later if there is an argument, even if it had nothing to do with race.

DEATH: No one gets out of the world alive. I heard in a sermon the a few months back, "we all have an expiration date," so it is important what you do with your time in the world. The good news is: LOVE NEVER DIES!

The *loss* of loved ones is, in my opinion, the most emotionally painful life events we will experience. The death of a child is one of the most difficult since parents do not expect to outlive children. There is no measure for emotional pain. Each of us feels differently and we all experience it differently.

There are seven stages to grief:

1 Shock

2 Denial

3 Anger

4 Bargaining (usually with God)

5 Guilt

6 Depression

7 Acceptance.

These stages can come and go, or we can experience them simultaneously. If we get stuck in any one stage, the thing to do is to seek out a grief therapist. There is no time limit on grief. If you hear "you should be over this by now," please keep in mind that we are all unique and that is not the truth. We all process the loss of a loved one in our own time.

Death of family or friends, even deaths we hear about in the news can bring thoughts of our own mortality, which for some of us is a scary thought. If a fear of death seems to preoccupy your thoughts, talk it over with an older relative or a therapist so that you can put things in proper perspective.

Our loved ones do not want us to waste our lives "stuck" in grief mode for them. Many have appeared to loved ones in dreams, (the easiest way for the Spirit World to contact us) or they have been told when seeing a Medium their loved one does not want them to feel sad or to suffer. It is my belief that we will see our loved ones after our own death, but that does not mean we should in any way try to hurry things along to be with them.

Many people have thoughts of suicide at one time or another in their lives, it is not as abnormal as it feels to us. It is my belief that, our soul comes into the world for a purpose. Life is the classroom for the soul and I believe that the soul continues on after death. If we cut this life short to stop the pain we feel, it is my belief that we (our soul) will be born again to face the same lessons. I suggest that if it is the truth (as I believe it is), why take a chance on repeating all the lessons you have already conquered? Please seek professional help. Thoughts of suicide do not mean that you are "crazy",. Such thoughts do mean that you are in pain and therapists understand that very well and can help. See Chapters D—Dying, S—Suicide.

DECADES: Each decade of our lives carries its own special challenges, lessons and rewards. At 20, we take everything very seriously, sometimes too seriously and this can be a very painful time for us. As we mature and learn that worry will only give us more to worry about, we can learn to be happy with where we are in life. As long as you take care of yourself and your body, you will be amazed at how good you feel, whether you are 20, 40, 60, or older.

DENIAL: Denial seems to go hand in hand with addiction. Refusing to honestly look at the obvious (that everyone else sees), is a safety net against having to take responsibility and change. Most people are in denial because they don't really want to change. They refuse to or are unable to take an honest look at the situation that needs changing and worse, they do NOT want to change the behavior that common sense tells them is no good for them. Too often there has to be a painful, rock bottom time reached, before one awakens from a serious case of denial. That is not to say that we MUST hit rock bottom, we have the free will to make good, conscious, decisions for ourselves anytime we are ready.

Any action or substance that causes us to numb pain, fear, or other emotions, can set us up for denial. Do not sabotage yourself by denying there is a problem, instead, be willing to meet challenges head on and deal with them. If a loved one or friend tells you one day, that you are in denial of something, pay attention. Do not be ashamed to seek out professional help if it is available to you. A strong Spiritual Path is a great help with denial and addictions. See also Chapter A—Addiction.

DEPRESSION: We all have life events that are sad. Depression is getting stuck in the sadness (it can also be a chemical imbalance). I've also read that it is "anger turned inward". It can take many forms. A common form is sleeping too much. If you recognize the symptoms of depression, don't attempt to just wait it out for it to get better, it usually doesn't go away on its own. Seek help from a trusted doctor, get therapy and find the right spiritual path for yourself pronto! I am very much against prescribing anti-depressants for people without ordering group therapy or counseling. If your doctor just prescribes the drugs and doesn't tell you to get counseling, ASK for it~.

When a person is depressed, it often feels like life just isn't going to or cannot get any better. That thinking reinforces the depression and at times it will feel as if there is a gigantic hole waiting for you to fall into. The many people I know who worked their way out of depression did it when they: "were sick and tired, of being sick and tired".

It has been said and I do believe that most human crises have roots in spiritual crises. I believe forgiveness is the bottom line to the anger and/or sadness that one carries with them everyday, including forgiveness of the self. See Chapter F—Forgiveness.

DETACHMENT: We have been given the whole world to enjoy, learn from and leave in better shape. It is so easy to be attached to our careers, material possessions or people in our lives; but it is best to not be too attached to any animal, feeling, person, place or thing. I believe we are granted the use of them but should not be so attached we cannot imagine doing or living without them. We should enjoy all aspects of our lives and each chapter or decade with the spirit of unconditional love and not just for selfish purposes, only interested in one's own agenda.

When we leave this world, we take nothing and no one with us, although I do believe we will meet again those we love. Its good to remember we are Spiritual Beings having a Human Experience and we are here to let our light shine and to learn to love unconditionally.

Years ago, I noticed that "things" I really liked would get broken; so I asked my teacher about it. She told me that I was learning detachment!

DIVINE ORDER: Divine order is a state of being, where every aspect of our lives is in order. "Mine sure isn't," you might be thinking; well I say: "Fake it till you make it" Put on your "Grace Face", smile more. Greet each day with the thought "Today is the first day of the rest of my life, it is Glorious!" Before you know it, your life will be in Divine Order!

Of course you are the one who has to do the work to clean and shape up your life. Declaring Divine Order, invites the highest and best of spiritual vibrations to flow in your life. Affirm: "My life and affairs are in Divine Order", when you feel the way isn't clear. A light will shine and you will see the way. Once you reach your 50's you will begin to recognize pieces as they fall in order, or learn to recognize the threads in your life's tapestry.

DIVINE SELF: Divine order is a state of being, where every aspect of our lives is in order. "Mine sure isn't," you might be thinking; well I say: "Fake it till you make it" Put on your "Grace Face", smile more. Greet each day with the thought "Today is the first day of the rest of my life, it is Glorious!" Before you know it, your life will be in Divine Order!

Of course you are the one who has to do the work to clean and shape up your life. Declaring Divine Order, invites the highest and best of spiritual vibrations to flow in your life. Affirm: "My life and affairs are in Divine Order", when you feel the way isn't clear. A light will shine and you will see the way. Once you reach your 50's you will begin to recognize pieces as they fall in order, or learn to recognize the threads in your life's tapestry.

DIVORCE: In years gone by and earlier generations people would stay married no matter how poorly they got along. In these more modern times, divorce is very common experience for many of us. I do not advocate staying together "for the sake of the kids" while everyone is miserable. If you realize that the person you married is not right for you, do what you need to do to make a fresh start and let that be okay. What was once a powerful love can turn out to be a destructive force in our lives. Also, if one person grows and the other does not, its not really anyone's "fault." Someone who is right for us at point in our life may not be right for us later on.

Divorce is always easier to deal with if it is your own choice. Often divorce carries a sense of failure, so this is a good time to seek therapy or find a self-help book to help you cope, and reinforce that you made the right decision. If you find yourself at the point of divorce, accept your decision and let it be okay.

Divorce is not the most pleasant of experiences, but there are times when it is necessary. It is important if our relationship fails to move on, not only knowing but accepting that it is the best for all concerned.

When our spouse leaves us for another, it is a major challenge to move on. There are support groups and therapists who can help you to deal with this change in your life. It is important that we do not move forward with bitterness in our heart. If someone leaves you or chooses another, it is really their loss, not yours.

It is not worth the time and effort to be in a relationship with a cheater or otherwise dishonest person. Human beings do make mistakes. If they are not dishonest the relationship is worth saving and working on. Some use the excuse it "just happened," I believe "we all have free will, life doesn't just happen to us, we do make choices."

For the sake of the children born of a relationship that is failing, commit to loving each other enough to be friendly and continue raising your children. They do not always get a vote when it comes to divorce. Do not be afraid to seek professional help for the entire family, it will benefit everyone in the years to come.

DRESS: The American society puts a lot of emphasis on being slim and sexy dressing. Dressing modestly is the best thing we can do for ourselves. It does make its own statement. We can be sexy without showing everything we have. Our Middle Eastern Indian sisters, and other cultures favor long, colorful and flowing garments which are quite beautiful as are the ladies who wear them.

When we dress sexy, we get the interest of others in a sexual way, there isn't a lot of respect that comes with that. It may be old fashioned, but dressing and leaving some things to the imagination is good. If you attract a man with a sexy outfit you get someone who wants sex, if you attract a man with your inner beauty, you attract someone interested in who you are.

DRUGS: There are some wonderful, lifesaving drugs on the market and there are some life destroying drugs out there too. Our Society seems to be a quick fix society. We've all seen commercials where a doctor says: "take two aspirin and call me in the morning". Many people would like to think they can take a pill and their pain will go away. That is just not the truth. While tranquilizers and pain pills can be a great blessing in a crisis, the only way out of inner pain is to work through it and get past it.

It is unbelievably easy to become addicted to pain killers or other prescription drugs and then be in denial of a problem because a doctor prescribed them. We have heard of people going to several doctors for pain killers. If you acknowledge that you have this problem in your life seek out rehabilitative help, face your inner pain, get over it and get on with life. There is truly a beautiful world if we are conscious enough to see it and not attempting to escape it. There is a lot to be said for the miracle of life and the Divine Spirits we are.

DYING: I look at dying as making a transition from life as we know it, to life in the Spiritual world also known as heaven. A Near Death Experience (NDE) at age 25, showed me with certainty that there is an "after life" or a very busy and real, Spiritual Realm that is like visiting a busy city. If you believe that it is "all over" when we die, you will be in for a rude awakening. Often we hear at funeral's, "well they are at peace now" or, "they aren't suffering". That is true, for there is no suffering in the spirit world, only love and peace, but the soul goes on for more lessons and growth.

In the Bible it says: "In My Father's House there are many mansions." What the NDE showed me is that there are many levels to heaven, or "mansions." We go to the level we have earned by the life we have lived. As long as we are breathing, we can change the life we are living and strive to live a "Spiritual Life."

Generations ago it must have been very difficult for people who knew they were dying, because no one talked about it in front of, or with them. Today there are many caring people who will put aside their own fears and discuss death openly with a loved one or friend. Sometimes the best thing we can do is be with and listen to them. Not only will you feel better, but they will also. There are now many good hospice programs to assist us during this transition. Find out what is available to you locally. A good book to read is one by Author Betty Eady, "Embraced by the Light".

DYSFUNCTIONAL: It is a sad fact that many families, whether single parented or with both parents in the home are dysfunctional. We probably pass dysfunction down from generation to generation until someone declares "no more" and decides to change it by getting a grip and teaching their young in a life affirming and loving way. There are many self help books available or please seek counseling to break this cycle. See Chapter A—Abuse.

CHAPTER E

Eating Disorders, Ego, Empty Nest Syndrome, Enjoyment, Escapism, Etheric Body, Ethics.

EATING DISORDERS: Eating disorders are emotional disorders. We are either trying to feed a hungry heart, or trying to starve one. Realize your Divine Self, get a working relationship going with the Creator, from whom you are a Divine Spark; commit to love yourself, a day at a time. Don't be ashamed to seek therapy for this problem, as soon as you recognize it in yourself or your children. Many famous people have successfully conquered this problem and so can you.

Most of the trouble we get into with overeating starts with what we feed our young children. Too many well meaning parents give young children candy, donuts and other sweets as a "treat". Young children love apple slices with peanut butter as much as any junk food. Please think about what you are feeding your young and what it will do to them later. Of course that means you have to get healthy and change your eating habits too.

Ego: As defined in Worldbook Encyclopedia: "EGO, is a term used in psychoanalysis to describe one of the three parts of the mind. The two other parts are the id, or instincts, and the superego, or conscience." The ego resolves conflicts; the individual's instinctual impulses, his or her sense of guilt, and the demands of external reality.

For example, the ego regulates emotions and impulses that might not be acceptable to other people. The ego also governs such areas as memory, thought and decision making, walking and other voluntary movements, and perceptions, such as hearing, feeling, and sight.

Psychoanalysts use the word ego to mean a person's self. In popular usage, the word has come to mean selfishness, self-love, or self-esteem. Obviously Ego is not a bad thing, but too much of it stuck in a negative area certainly is. Especially if we believe we are a gift to the planet and all we come in contact with, and don't believe the same about everyone else. I believe that one of life's lessons is to conquer Ego and live in an unconditional loving space. See Chapters D—Detachment, G—Greed.

EMPTY NEST SYNDROME: After we faced all the joys, trials and tribulations of having our children and growing up with them, the next and huge "rite of passage" having to do with parenthood is they grow up and leave home. Depending on how many children you have, it might come in gradually, like the layers in an onion, or can happen all at once; one day your "purpose" was to take care of your family, then you find yourself standing alone and wondering where to go from here. In my case, it hit me all at once, and I cried buckets of tears; I felt that all I *knew* well was motherhood and my cry was okay, now what do I do? This is the time for a personal inventory. List all that you know and all that you have accomplished and you will discover many talents beyond motherhood. It is time to redirect your energy. If you feel that you don't have anything to list, it is the time to enroll in school for something you have been interested in. In other words, don't sit and cry, take stock, set a goal and GET GOING.

If you find that you cannot stop crying or are very depressed, please talk to your doctor. There is no stigma in getting help for something every other Mom has had to face. Do remember to give yourself a pat on the back for raising children is the toughest job in the world. Guess what? After the tears are dried, and you've found out what's coming next, you learn that "averages" dictate that your child will return home up to 3 times before they finally fly; you think you're *done*, then they bring you their babies and the cycle begins again. See Chapters A—Achieving Goals, L—Letting Go.

ENJOYMENT: The root word is *Joy*. Give yourself permission to enjoy your life. Smile more, laugh heartily and don't take everything so seriously. Years from now, people might not remember what you did, but they will remember what you said. Harsh words can play over and over again to the person you said them to. Strive to be pleasant in all circumstances. Give yourself permission to relax and enjoy the life you have made for yourself. See Chapter J—Joy.

ESCAPISM: What I call any action or substance that causes us to numb pain, fear, or not feel our emotions. Do not choose to sabotage yourself further by denying there is a problem, instead, be willing to meet challenges and emotions head-on and deal with them; do not be ashamed to seek out professional help if it is available to you. If it is not available, at least go check out the self-help books, there are many good ones out today. A strong Spiritual Path is a great help with escapism by teaching us how to live in the here and now. Life is not a race to be won, but a journey to be savored. See Chapter A—Addiction, D—Denial.

ETHERIC BODY: We are far more than our physical bodies; the physical is the one we are most familiar with. The second body is like condensed smoke, it is energy. The first body is solid. The second body is just like the first as far as shape is concerned, but it is not solid. Practice feeling your energy body by holding one hand about three inches over the other; slowly bring the hand down until you feel the energy on the other hand; then practice on various parts of your body. Once familiar with your energy, practice on friends or loved ones, even pets. Can you see the energy field around a bush or a tree? It's an exciting discovery and a life long study. See Chapter M—Metaphysics.

ETHICS: Ethics and Morals are cousins. It is a good thing to be the sort of person who has both ethics and morals. These are qualities we choose much as a criminal chooses to do a crime. Our Country has had many excellent role models.

If you are not sure what high ethics or high morals are about, check the history of both government and religious Masters and Saints.

Once you decide that you are going to live the best life possible and strive daily to live it, make a list of your own, personal, Code of Ethics; many websites and businesses list their Mission or Vision Statements, make your own, print yourself a copy and read it often as a reminder. See Chapters G—Golden Rule, M—Morals.

CHAPTER F

Faith, **F**airy tales, **F**amily, **F**ear, **F**lirting, **F**orgiveness, **F**orties, **F**riends, **F**un

FAITH: Faith is the substance of things hoped for, the essence of things unseen. Faith is like an unused muscle, if we never use it, it is weak; the more we exercise it, the stronger it becomes. Faith is the ability to trust in self, family, and Creator or Diety you serve, that one is loved and all will be well. Realizing one's own Divinity frees the ability to use faith. We get tests of faith during each decade of our lives, so that we are able to affirm or grow in faith.

I am reminded of something I heard in church or read, I no longer remember who said or wrote it, but it is to the effect that: When we put our faith in man, our faith is in the wrong place. When we lift our faith to our Creator, all else seems to fall in place. I have found that to be true in my own life. We are human beings having a spiritual experience. Our home is in the heavens when our lessons here are done.

FAIRY TALES: Too many of us bought into the *happily ever after* wording of the fairy tales. It seemed like Magic, That without any real effort on our part, all will be okay. The fairy tales neglected to tell us that ALL relationships take determination, and WORK and sometimes, no matter how hard we have tried, we do not "live happily ever after," and will experience times of sadness. See Chapter F—Faith.

FAMILY: On a conscious level we don't get to choose the group of people we are born into. We can choose to adopt others along the way we feel close to and they become our extended family. When families adopt a child, that child becomes as much a family member as those born in the family. Strong family love and ties are among life's greatest blessings.

How wonderful it is to hear someone say: "my mother, father, sister, brother, or other relative, is my best friend." Everyone born or adopted into the family deserves care, good role models and unconditional love and the respect of other family members.

Just as genetics is passed along, so are some of the same challenges, i.e., alcoholism, drug use, other addictions, mannerisms, physical characteristics and medical problems.

There are many warm, loving families in society, but sadly, there are also many dysfunctional families who hurt each other. The bottom line to those hurts is forgiveness (that doesn't mean forgive them and invite them to dinner) and requires that we consciously work to stop negative tapes from playing over and over in our minds. When a memory comes up, over something a family member said or did to hurt you, do a "cancel, cancel" to the thought; say a forgiveness mantra and understand in your heart, that when they know better they will do better. Note: that doesn't mean going back for more; just means you allow yourself to be at peace. See Chapter F—Forgiveness.

What if you find yourself in this world without too much family, or perhaps with no living family members? Start where you are, in my case I felt like a tree with 3 tiny branches (my 3 children) after years of care, the branches have tripled themselves (my 9 grandchildren) and I am anything but lonely! What I am telling you is that what appears to be the situation now, will not stay that way. There is a bigger picture! Life is a tapestry that we do not see fully until the weaving is done.Be friendly and friends will come into your life and feel just like "family".

FEAR: Fear can sometimes paralyze us to the point we cannot get going even when in a desperate situation. Fear is a valid human emotion whose purpose is to keep us out, or get us out of danger. A good affirmation when one is fearful of something is: I am Pure Spirit and Spirit does not fear. That will help calm you as you figure out what your next move should be. Faith is the opposite of fear, and as I have often said, "Faith is like an unused muscle, if you do not use it, it is weak; the more you use it, the stronger it becomes". If you find that much of your time is spent living in fear, please talk to a therapist, or Pastor.

FLIRTING: Flirting is a big part of the *human condition* It can be harmless, but can spell disaster for those committed to other people, bringing about devastating consequences to the mate or family. Responsible flirting, that harms no one else, is fun for the single population, but for the committed person one is wise not to flirt with other people. Practice flirting at home and allow yourself to really get into that.

Once what I call the "honeymoon phase" is over, and dirty dishes and socks appear, one must make a conscious effort to remain "in love" with the other person and not take them or the relationship for granted. Smile a lot at your partner, and they will smile back at you! Get creative about ways to remain in love as though you are still "honeymooning". Most of all, do not take your partner for granted, tend to each other with joy and love will continue to bloom. See Chapter A—Angels.

FORGIVENESS: Forgiveness is a gift you give to yourself! If we have experienced abuse of any sort, any "hits to the heart or core of ourselves" whether from the distant or more recent past, we must take a walk, on the forgiveness path. The main block to healing any dis-ease, whether in our Emotional, Physical or Spiritual bodies, lies in forgiveness. Abuse from another person or even from ourselves, constitutes a "hit to the heart."

The healing and release of that negative adrenaline, and block to our happiness, lies in forgiveness. You might be thinking by now, "What? And leave them off the hook?" It is important to remember that you are not in charge of judgment and punishment, there is a Higher Power in charge of that. Many of us grew up hearing "forgive and forget," those you heard it from had it half right, yes, we must forgive, there is no other way; however, we must acknowledge that we do

NOT forget! For our own peace of mind, so that we don't have to feel guilty because we just can't seem to forget or every time we remember something that hurt us, often we think, " Gee, I thought I forgave that." If you feel no pain when you remember something, then you have forgiven it; if you feel anger or pain, then more forgiveness work is necessary.

Our subconscious processes the info, the good, the bad, and the ugly, on an indiscriminate basis; to will ourselves to forget means that we might forget the good too. A test of that would be to take a mental walk, during the roughest times of your life and look for the good also present, can you remember it? Our subconscious mind does not fail to hear us, but does not discriminate what we tell it, so, just tell yourself to forgive from now on.

Once we have forgiven something, the memory or flashback will carry less and less pain; after a while, there simply is no pain as you view that scene of your life. It is like watching an old familiar movie. Forgiveness is a process, it rarely happens after we have said "I forgive you," it has to be worked on. Memories will come up for review, remind yourself that you choose to forgive that.

To walk a path of joy in this life, in this moment in time, is to choose not to carry bitterness, anger, guilt, pain, or sorrow, in our emotional backpacks. All of the mentioned negatives, or any ONE of them by itself, promotes "distorted thinking." Distorted thinking blocks love and light. *We* are the only doctor that can cure our negative or distorted thinking; we are the only ones who can stop playing the negative tapes ingrained in our subconscious. Just like the surgeons have surgical tools, dentists use dental tools, human beings have a forgiveness tool.

Walking the forgiveness path isn't easy at first! But with practice, you skip from one step to the next and can move right along in love. Yes, there was pain. We ALL have had at least some pain in life, overcoming that pain is also a big part of the overall lesson. We come into life to face and learn lessons, life is a classroom for the soul.

I have a short Forgiveness Prayer (author unknown) that I

learned many years ago, it helps me walk the forgiveness path. It goes like this:

I FULLY AND FREELY FORGIVE YOU,
I LOOSE YOU AND LET YOU GO,
ON YOUR WAY NOW,
TO YOUR HIGHEST GOOD,
AS I GO ON TO MINE.
It is done, It is done, IT IS DONE!
(Metaphysical Law of 3)
and I AM GRATEFUL-

Remember, Forgiveness is not condoning the actions of another or, meant to invalidate your feelings. Forgiveness is about getting free of the pain, turning the judgment and punishment over to a Higher Power. In our forgiveness work, we might feel anger at the other person or situation, that is OKAY; it just means that forgiveness hasn't happened yet. In consistently working on forgiveness, it does happen. You will still have the memory of that person or event, but it will be pain free; like watching an old, familiar movie.

"Forgiveness is not the misguided act of condoning irresponsible, hurtful behavior. Nor is it a superficial turning of the other cheek that leaves us feeling victimized and martyred. Rather it is the finishing of old business that allows us to experience the present, free of contamination from the past" Joan Borysenko, Ph.D., Fire in the Soul.

"Forgiveness cancels the conditions in the mind that are blocking the full flow of love or life energy. Forgiveness is independent of the behavior of others. It is a free personal choice and an act of free will." (Author unknown)

Forgiveness is a gift you give yourself; it doesn't mean invite the person to dinner or to hurt you again. If you choose to continue to be with this person, then allow the things that happened to be gone from you by releasing them when a memory or flashback comes, tell yourself "no,"that is over, I will not allow it to continue to hurt us." Invite the Angels in charge of love into your relationship daily (every 4 hrs). Mistakes are made, lessons learned, and a better way can be found to treat each other. When we know better, we do better! We need not be in charge of judgment and punishment, there is a higher power in charge of that. :-)

Charles Fillmore, founder of Unity (also known as Unity School of Christianity), said that: "sitting quietly for 30 minutes a day, forgiving anything and anyone who comes to mind can cure ANY ill known to man or woman.

The final most important thing to know about forgiveness is that, we MUST learn to forgive ourselves as often and as quickly as possible. When we know better, we do better- There is NO point in beating ourselves up for what we perceive to be our *mistakes*. It's all part of the lessons our soul came here to learn.

What about those of us who attempt to forgive something and are still in relationship with the person who hurt or abused us? Again, understanding that we DO NOT forget, we have to do something with the thoughts when they pop back into our minds. Those of you who are prayerful, might say a prayer. Memorize the forgiveness mantra, it will come in handy, and should be said again immediately as a memory or flashback comes to mind.

Another tool would be to stop right then and there, take a few seconds to write down 5 things you are grateful for. It will IMMEDIATELY change your energy. Forgiveness is a matter of conditioning ourselves, through CONSCIOUS EFFORT, let the memories come (and they will) but taking action to counteract the negatives with a positive tool, allows us to cope as we build the future we desire.

FORTIES: Life truly does begin in the 40's, but I don't believe it begins AT 40. The years between 42 and 45, bring MUCH growth, especially if one is interested in Metaphysics or Spirituality. It is the time of life when so much comes together. I believe, it is the reason for the "life begins at 40" theme. If a person is not particularly interested in Metaphysics (study of beyond the physical), when the opportunity presents itself to heal old issues, it will be missed. Many chances will be presented to learn; do not be close minded or afraid to deal with the issues. Much of the growth is very awesome and carries a-ha moments. The ages between 42 and 45 present much growth and opportunities to heal old wounds and really tighten up any self esteem issues. Please note, some of the healing will feel very painful at times and it is okay to cry. See Chapter T—Tears.

This is also the time when the "mid-life crises" comes (approximately at age 45, although some experience it at 42, still others will be late bloomers). How well you deal with the aftermath of the mid-life crises, depends upon how well you have learned to forgive yourself if you feel you made a mistake. See Chapters F—Forgiveness, M—Metaphysics.

FRIENDS: True friends are among life's greatest treasures and a valuable asset; they will uplift and support you, false friends can cause you to slip into life's muddy waters; choose yours carefully. Too often we take more care shopping for clothes than we do evaluating those we think are friends. When you first meet someone, give yourself a chance to get to know them before trusting them with your most intimate sharing.

In order to have a friend, you must be willing to be a friend. If you want more friends in your life, be more friendly. Being friendly does not mean allow the other person to use us, (or we to use them), but equal give and take. A good friend will offer to help you when no one else will.

What makes friendships so neat, is that most often when one is down, the other person is up and thus we continue to uplift and support those we love as friends, and they us. Our friendships are emotional bonds that can last a lifetime, a soulmate connection that is a gift to us and we a gift to them. Our spouses and partners can know we are going through something, but our friends really understand what we go through in our daily lives.

FROGS: Also known as Fools, Punks, Drunks and Skunks! My Grandmother used to say: "You'll kiss a lot of frogs before the prince comes along", I didn't understand that as a young girl, but now, as a Grandmother myself, do I ever understand it (smile)! Learn to recognize a frog before you fall in love and you will save yourself a lot of wasted time and major heartache. It boils down to not being so lonely or wanting love that you latch onto the first person (or second, third or fourth) person that comes along and shows interest in you.

The stronger your self esteem, the more able you will be to resist making poor choices in relationships. See Chapter S—Self Esteem.

FUN: Too often we are so caught up in daily living, career, financial worries, etc., and we do not take time to have fun. Laughter is the best medicine it's said, and that is true. Children know how to have fun, join yours in play. If you don't have children yourself, go visit your relatives or friends that do. Don't forget to do one nice thing for yourself everyday. If you are a person who cannot seem to relax, learn relaxation techniques; if you cannot relax, you will not feel that your life is too much fun.

Learn to smile more, smiles are contagious and someone will smile back at you. Make a conscious effort to see the beauty in your life, and you will be able to relax and enjoy it! See Chapter G—Grounding.

CHAPTER G

Giving, Golden Rule, Gratitude, Greed, Grief,Grip, Grounding, Growth, Guilt

GIVING: It is a Universal Law that when we give freely, we receive freely also. If you think you have *nothing* to give, give a friend a treasured book or a scarf, and go on from there. Random acts of kindness are an excellent way to give back kindness you have received. Give the gift of your time and love if you feel you have nothing to give, and before you know it, blessings will return to you! If a few more drivers on the road gave the gift of courtesy to each other, I believe there would be less "road rage".

GOLDEN RULE: Do unto others as you would have them do unto you. Think about it, you prefer to be treated with kindness and respect; so give that same kindness and respect to others.

GRATITUDE: The feeling of being thankful for blessings we have received in life and those, which we know we will still be blessed with in the future. When you feel the most "down" or your energy seems scattered, stop right then and there and write down 5 things you are grateful for; It will immediately change your energy! Keeping a Gratitude Journal will help you to focus on how much is right instead of what is wrong. An attitude of gratitude, will keep the blessings flowing into your life.

GREED: A not so great quality and if one recognizes it in themselves, it is an excellent idea to change. Greed can take several forms, possessions, money, food, sex, you name it.

"You can't take it with you," is a very true statement. There is enough abundance in the world for everyone and all to share. See Chapters D—Detachment, E—Ego, G—Giving.

GRIEF: There are 7 stages to grief. Grieving is important, and we are given tears as a release. If we feel stuck in one of the stages, it is important to seek out grief counseling. The *loss* of loved ones is the most emotionally painful life events we will experience. The death of a child is one of the most difficult to face, since no one expects to outlive their children. It is my belief that love never dies. There is no measure for emotional pain, no right or wrong; each of us feels and experiences it differently, in our own time. There are seven known stages to grief:

1- Shock
2- Denial
3- Anger
4- Bargaining (usually with God)
5- Guilt
6- Depression
7- Acceptance

I believe there could be 8—Abandonment placed after guilt. If we get stuck in any one stage, the thing to do is to seek out a grief therapist; or check with local hospitals, many offer grief workshops or groups; you can also check with some of the well known disease societies, like Cancer Society, they usually offer brochures or information on grief recovery. The thing to remember when you hear "time heals all wounds" that each of us are not on the same timetable and what one person might get over in a year, can take another perfectly normal, human five years. A very harsh thing to say to a grieving person is: "You should be over this by now."Please refrain from saying that to a friend or relative. There is no timetable for "over". The Master teacher, Jesus Christ taught us to: "Love One Another"; Reiki Healing teaches us: To Do No Harm. Let us be loving and kind to one another.

Our loved ones do not want us to waste our lives "stuck" in grieving for them. Many have appeared to loved ones in dreams to let them know that, still others have gone to a Medium, hoping for a message from a loved one, and they are told that their loved one is fine and concerned about them.

In life we have many reasons to grieve, not only the loss of a loved one. It could be the loss of a job, a way of life we are used to, or just something that makes us sad. Remember to be gentle with yourself. See Chapters A—Abandonment, T—Tears.

GRIP: I'm sure you have heard at least once in your life "get a grip"! There is far too much mental illness in our Society. Many are truly ill, others are convinced they are because they don't fit the "norm". Yoga helps integrate Mind, Body and Spirit.

There are many wonderful herbs and herbal teas, which can help one stay calm and maintain an inner sense of well-being. The Herb, Ginkgo Biloba, is always promoted for memory, however it is not well known that Ginkgo also seems to "promote an inner feeling of well-being." as a friend once said to me. Flower Remedies are also good calming agents. . Sometimes, when stress abounds, you've just got to "hang onto your hat", life in a mental institution is no fun at all. Before you ask for tranquilizers to help you cope, practice eating healthy foods and learn the benefits of drinking herbal teas. See Chapter B—Bach Flower Remedies

GROUNDING: It takes approximately 3—4 weeks of daily practice to "get" this technique once learned, you can ground anytime. Anywhere, in a matter of seconds. I also call this: awakening to the spiritual self. Prior to attempting to meditate, begin to practice the following:

To awaken to the spiritual self that we are, we begin first by realizing who we are; we are spiritual beings having a human experience. We begin to learn to greet each other with the Namaste greeting. A Sanskrit word it means:

I honor the place in you in which the entire universe dwells...

I honor the place in you that is of truth...of love...And of light...

When you are in that place in you and I am in that place in me,

We are one, Namaste (na mas te)

We can practice on ourselves that greeting, extending to all in our life circle. We can instantly ground ourselves no matter where we are or what we are doing with the following easy technique:

Please note: this is not meditation, nor should it be used as such. This is a simple technique to use, when you are in need of calming or to get a grip when stress threatens to throw you in a tizzy. Sitting in a straight back chair, this can also be done in an auto, on a plane, while walking (after some practice) or any other vehicle whereby our feet are in a downward position. So that takes care of bikes, motorcycles, etc.

If you already know about the chakra energy centers, this will be a bit easier for you to grasp. If you do not know of chakras, they are spiritual energy centers located throughout the body. There are major and minor chakras. For our purposes, however we need only to know that we have 2 minor chakras located at the bottom of each foot, right below the ball of the foot, in the very center.

These two chakras are pointed straight downwards from our foot just like a tree whose roots are deep into mother earth; no matter how high we are actually above the earth we can ground our energy (We could be on the moon and still accomplish this technique).

Sitting in a straight backed chair close off the energy field—by putting our hands on our thighs; cupping them slightly, and connect thumb and forefinger; our energy field is now closed; through the two foot chakras we release the pent up energy, deep into mother earth.

With grounding, we feel calmer immediately. After becoming familiar with this technique, and with much practice and when in tune, you may begin to feel the sensitive energy areas, (chakras) and that makes grounding even easier.

We have above our heads a vortex of light (similar to a halo) this is from our crown chakra—located about six inches above the head, in the area of a baby's soft spot. For our purposes, we will visualize two kinds of light rings. One is white—above that, golden.

We learn to breathe stress away by breathing in a calm and unhurried way. Begin by taking in a long, cool, breath—in through the nostrils to the count of 8; feel your lungs expanding—feel the coolness of this breath...the healing coolness as it cools the fire's within you. Hold your breath to the count of 8—do as many numbers as your untrained lungs will let you—Release your breath to the count of eight, slowly, out of your mouth, releasing all "hot, angry, tired, air," and toxins lurking there.

Repeat this exercise till you get it right, and calming your self becomes second nature to you. Now that we are calm, and peaceful, we know that the light energy we are infilling with thru the top of our head—the golden/white energy is now flowing downward—throughout our body. At the same time—all negativity is being pushed straight out of the bottom of our feet deep into mother earth, where she can best dispose of and transmute the energy for recycling.

We are also pushing out of ourselves, any *dis ease*, depression or stress that we are dealing with. We are now grounded; and we allow that light to surround us. It is our protection as we go about our daily life. We are serene, dignified and graceful in our thoughts and action. We only need to remember this light and that it is available to us at anytime to reground ourselves no matter what is going on. Today is the first day of the rest of our lives, we can begin now to practice this and reach a new level of serenity in our daily living. We need to make this connection about once every 4 hours—more often during times of crises or stress.An excellent closing affirmations would be:**I AM a radiant being of light** or **I AM pure spirit and spirit is love.**

I wrote these grounding techniques 1/24/98, and have passed them on to many people, feel free to teach them to those you love. The younger we are when we learn to ground and center ourselves the better able we are to cope with everyday life.

GROWTH: I am not talking about physical growth but soul growth; I do so love "light bulb moments," and wondrous growth that feels like energy is in the air. Some growth takes us right out of pain into a place of acceptance or happiness in a very short period of time and we feel as though we have lost physical weight. We start the growth process at the moment of conception, our growth on the physical plane ends at the time of death. Growth continues on to infinity in the evolution of the Soul until we are all Masters. We learn throughout our entire lives and the saying "we learn something new everyday" is the truth, welcome growth!

GUILT: The awful feeling we have when we know we have done harm, others can make us feel we can't do anything right until we believe that ourselves. We can be our own harshest judge and jury. It is important to understand that all human beings make mistakes. It is necessary to learn how to forgive ourselves as quickly and as often as necessary when we feel we have made a mistake. My belief is that many of our "mistakes" are actually lessons we must experience for the growth of our souls. When we know better we do better! It is IMPERATIVE that whenever you feel the most guilt about something, you work on forgiving yourself and building self esteem. You were not born to fail! See Chapters F—Forgiveness, Chapter S—Self Esteem.

CHAPTER H

Happiness, **H**arm, **H**ard Headed, **H**ate, **H**ealing, **H**ealth, **H**erbs, **H**indsight, **H**urt, **H**ygiene

HAPPINESS: Happiness is not only a feeling that comes to us from other people or worldly events, about 50% of our happiness comes from those sources. Happiness is also a state of being. Anyone can learn "the skill of happiness" as we go about our daily lives; that is truly, the lasting kind of happiness. A strong foothold on a Spiritual Path shows us how to capture and hold the feeling of happiness on a daily basis. The affirmation: I AM Pure Spirit and all is well, can be of great help in teaching yourself to be happy from the inside out. The natural state of men and women is joy. See Chapter J—Joy,

HEALING: We are blessed in America and other parts of the world to have many great men and women doctors. Medical science makes tremendous advances in healing constantly. Nonetheless, we do have a responsibility and the ability to heal ourselves and others. Self Healing is a gift you can give yourself through the study of other forms of healing such as attunement to Reiki Healing (pronounced Ray Key). Reiki 1 is self healing. The first mandate for anyone interested in healing others is: **Healer, Heal Thyself!**

There are many alternative or complimentary means of healing available to us besides Reiki Healing. Anyone can heal others, whether by laying on of hands or distance healing; intent is everything.

The important thing to remember is that you, by yourself

are a channel for healing energy. Only God or your Diety does the actual healing. If you feel or are told that you have healing hands, seek out a qualified teacher; learn anatomy and study the body as much as possible. If you have an interest in healing yourself and others, you will be charged with the Mission: "Go and heal the World one person at a time"; teach others to heal and you will reach the masses. While you are studying the body, learn to become a lightworker for the spirit. See Chapters L—Light Worker, R—Reiki and Reflexology.

HEALTH: A healthy body and mind is what we strive for (or should). Health isn't usually that important to us until we get older and start to lose what we have taken for granted for so long. Then we begin to realize how important it is (or was).

It is good to take responsibility for our health and not depend on the doctors to fix whatever is wrong. We are a "quick fix" society, preferring to take a pill and have it be all better. We fail to realize that we need to take responsibility for our health and WORK at keeping it good; Even if we get to this awareness after a major illness, it is never too late to start right where you are to prevent further deterioration.

Exercise is very important to the care and keeping of the human body. Even if it does not appeal to you, get involved with a fitness program; once you start, you will find that it actually does energize you and you will find yourself wanting to do it; its wonderful how that works! If you aren't taking especially good care of your health, understand that when we enter our 30's and beyond, our bodies will break down if we are not doing good nutrition and exercise to keep them healthy.If you experience a lot of joint or other pain, look into water arobics which is an excellent and painfree way to exercise. See Chapter H—Hygiene

HARD HEADED: We can get into big trouble being too hard headed to listen to others when they are attempting to give sound advice. A really old saying is this: "A hard head makes a soft ass"! In our family, we sometimes tease and say, you don't only have a hard head, but a brick (smile). We do need a certain amount of being hard headed or a certain amount of stubborness to accomplish goals that seem nearly impossible, and give us the perserverance to make it through, but I am talking about the type of hardheadedness that makes you ignore good advice or even that "small voice within" that says,, "you really shouldn't do that". See also Chapter C—Choices.

HARM: Causing injury or ill feelings, intentional or accidental pain to others. Harm can be emotional, mental, physical or spiritual. A good rule of thumb to live by: TO DO NO HARM. See Chapter A—Abuse

HATE: Hate is the opposite of love. We would all be a lot better off if no one in our society or world had feelings of bitterness or hatred. Stop the little children from saying: "I hate you" to brothers or sisters, or worse yet...to parents.

We have the right to not *like* someone or something, but no one has the right to hate anyone or anything. If you have been hurt by someone, forgiveness is the bottom line to the way out of pain. See Chapter F—Forgiveness.

HERBS: A good multi vitamin is a good place to start, but shouldn't be the end of supplements in your diet. There are many excellent reference books out on herbs. Take the time to check at least one out and to learn for yourself, which supplements might be right for you. Be sure and check with your doctor before starting any herbal regime. See Chapter V—Vitamins.

HINDSIGHT: In retrospect is 20/20. Now just what does that mean? Well, if you are not willing or unable to listen to others advice, when it's all said and done and you are living with the subsequent mess, you will have 20/20 vision about what you should have done! See Also Chapters C—Choices and H—Hard Headed.

HOMOSEXUALITY: It is still a debate whether homosexuality is "in the genes," formed by an overbearing mother or other caretaker, or a past life or karmic issue.

Too often, one will hear gay people refer to themselves as "faggots or dykes", worse yet, the old term "queer". Those words do not promote good inner feelings. As far as I am concerned, homosexuals are children of God and to be honored as well as any other human being; nonetheless, it isn't the easiest of lifestyles to live; harder even if a person is in "the closet" for fear of losing love and respect of family or friends. No matter who we are, not everyone will like us, nor will we like them; but those we love, and are good too will love us back.

Some families have a hard time accepting the choice of their loved one. It is my belief that no matter what the personal belief and choice of each person is, we still owe family members love, respect and acceptance.

HYGIENE: Too often, folks seem to be unconscious of good hygiene. If you stand in a public restroom it is appalling to see how many people do not wash their hands after using the bathroom. It can go downhill from there. None of us should tolerate fast food chains allowing employees to handle cash and then serve food, or vice versa, without plastic gloves. If you see that, report it to the local health department for the sake of all who patronize that restaurant.

The best thing for the care and keeping of the body is a daily shower and a bath at least once weekly, which soothes not only the body but the mind and allows us to not only get off dirt, but to clean our aura too. There are many great products on the market to take care of ourselves and any rough edges, go shopping! Interesting enough is that the higher our self esteem, the better care we take of ourselves. See Chapters B—Body, S—Self Esteem.

HURT: Sometimes, life hurts; buy some fun Band-Aids. See Chapter P—Pain

CHAPTER I

Identity, Illness, Inner Child, Intuition

IDENTITY: Awareness of who you are and what your life purpose is actually becomes a gift to yourself and is quite freeing. Identify what can harm you and steer clear of it. Write your own "code of ethics" and live by it. When something has to be changed, we can change our minds, set goals and get to work.

These days we hear a lot about "identity theft" learn all you can about protecting your family, even your babies against this crime. See also Chapters A—Achieving Goals and P—Purpose

ILLNESS: Rich or poor, we will all face some illness in our lifetime. I read on a billboard while driving one day: God lays us on our back to make us look up! For sure it will slow us down. Louise Hayes has a book that I love entitled: "You Can Heal Your Life". I do believe that thoughts are powerful and if we think we are ill, we will be. In her book, Louise lists many illnesses and the possible thinking behind the formation of a certain disease. Her book provides valuable insight.

In my opinion, there is nothing worse than feeling ill or being in pain much of the time. Often we will not get the sympathy and understanding of loved ones, since they just don't feel the particular pain themselves so are clueless. If that is the case for you, and you have a chronic illness, check out support groups for what you are dealing with. It will help and you might just meet some wonderful new friends. Nothing is quite as bad as it seems, if we can share our pain or sorrow with others. After all, we are all in the same boat in that we are dealing with "the human condition".

Some illness can be a cry for attention, such as hypochondria. If you feel or have heard from friends or relatives that they think you are a hypochondriac, seek professional help to get past it and get on with your life. See Chapter T—Tears.

INNER CHILD: We all have an "inner child" that has nothing to do with how old we actually are. Inside each of us is the child we once were, with the ability to feel wonderment and joy at the smallest of things. We all carry at least some painful baggage in our emotional backpacks. A fair portion comes directly from the treatment we received (or care we didn't get) as a young, impressionable child. It can take us half of our lives to overcome it. Some never do. They cling so tightly to the "victim" or "poor me" mode, and cling to feeling pretty sorry for themselves; or have learned to be angry and that becomes a habit.

Other times, the pain is swept "under the rug" or we "stuff" it; eventually there comes to be a short circuit between our heart, our brain and our ability to love ourselves and others. We all deal with pain in our own way. The problem with sweeping or stuffing, is that scar tissue builds up, and we act out, in many ways; addictions of all kinds; self destructive, self condemning or self sabotaging behavior and thoughts; even a strong amount of self hate.

If we just didn't get enough love in our childhood to give us the start we needed, what can change that? Commitment and conscious effort daily to stay focused on SELF LOVE, positive thoughts and goals.

Childhood is rough enough from the taunting some get from other children. If there wasn't a stable, loving home to come home to, the pain is worse and can fester for years to come. If there is emotional, physical or sexual abuse inflicted on children in the home, it can leave mental scars that require professional treatment, and carry over to the children we raise. If we don't have a good self esteem level, we cannot teach it to another. The good news is that we can change it for ourselves.

The bottom line to healing is love (self love) and forgiveness. If those caretakers or other children knew better, they would have done better; if we put ourselves in their shoes, going over their life experiences, for all we know we would have reacted to others in the same way; does that excuse their bad behavior? No, however, it is a fact that child abuse and family violence is a vicious cycle that is passed down from generation to generation until someone says: 'NO MORE."

Awareness is half the battle won. We still have to win the war. Once we realize (brain gets connected to the heart) that yes, we were hurt and we WANT to heal, we can recover, and find that joyful space in our heart that says, I CHOOSE to be whole. Choosing is the first step.

If we are lucky enough to heal childhood trauma BEFORE age 28, our soul is not wounded. If we cannot heal it, our pain becomes a wound our soul will get many other opportunities to heal. In cases of severe abuse, it appears to me that we can finally heal between the ages of 43 and 45. We have the mental maturity to be able to look at, forgive and heal the abuse and finally go about the business of our true purpose here on planet earth.

Life can begin at 40, but if we have not healed childhood trauma our life will continue to give painful opportunities to wake up and heal; Unfortunate are those souls who leave this earth in their 70's or 80's as bitter, unhappy people, who never experienced or allowed themselves to see the beauty in this world and who never knew more than a fleeting bit of happiness. For some, the pain is so great, they leave at a much earlier age (by their own hand) as bitter and unhappy as those who live much longer.

If you know that you were wounded in childhood, seek out a therapist who specializes in "Inner Child" work. There are many great self help books on the market today, especially "Healing the Child Within" by Charles Whitfield, and John Bradshaw, "Homecoming: Reclaiming and Championing Your Inner Child" as well as "Healing the Shame that binds you" and "Inner Child." See Chapters A—Abuse; J—Joy; H—Happiness; S—Self Esteem

INTUITION: The *feeling* we have that we *know* what is going to come about; i.e., Psychic Ability. EVERYONE has psychic ability; just varying degrees. One has to *trust* that their *gut* is giving them accurate information. We are all familiar with the term "women's intuition", that is psychic ability!

Not only women have a good intuition, many men have good intuition too. It is telling or warning you to pay attention to something; Learn to trust it, our *guts* often know things before the experience presents itself. It is real and not a figment of your imagination.

Some religions preach against psychic awareness but it is my belief that it is not an evil thing but a gift from a loving Creator. See also Chapter P—Psychic Ability.

CHAPTER J

Jealousy, Jewelry, Joy, Journaling, Judging others

JEALOUSY: At times, other's people's lives appear infinitely more attractive than our own; "The grass is always greener on the other side of the fence". Wanting what someone else has, without being willing to do the WORK they did to get where they are, is what I call "distorted thinking." Everything is available, to those who want to stay in school, or work toward success. The feeling that another human *belongs* to one person and cannot talk to or look at anyone else, is jealousy stemming from insecurity; work on self esteem. Love does not mean chaining a soul. A good portion of jealousy stems from fear and insecurity; fear that we are not good enough to hold or to keep our mate happy; or other fear that we are somehow inadequate. See Chapter S—Self Esteem.

JEWELRY: Precious metal carries vibrations; Turquoise has been treasured by many cultures around the world, hailed for its mystical and healing powers. Amethyst is also known for its spiritual and healing vibration. We hear "a diamond is forever". If no one gives you one, buy your own. It is a good idea to learn about the vibrations of gems and crystals. Wear those that resonate with your spirit, or contain the energy of qualities you would like to attract. Everyone should wear a clear quartz AND a rose quartz crystal near their heart. Clear quartz clears negativity and rose quartz is said to "heal the heart," and I've found that to work both inside and out. It is my opinion that it is good to wear a simple gold necklace worn around the neck since its metaphysical properties are to banish fear and negativity. Study the vibrations of precious stones and crystals, it is very interesting, not "new age" at all, because the art of jewelry making began in ancient times.

JOY: The natural state of Man and Woman is Joy! Love increases joy; the more love you have in your heart, the more joy you will have in your life and home. Angels are joyful beings. When you develop a personal relationship with Angels, joy will increase, as you see miracles happen right before your eyes. See Chapters A—Angels; H—Happiness.

JOURNALING: It seems to me that journaling has it roots in generations that kept diaries. Journaling is popular these days and an EXCELLENT way to put a life in the right direction. There is something to be said for the written word. We might not remember verbatim what you said, but the written word clearly leaves a lasting impression. If you aren't journaling yet, go to Oprah's Website and read about journaling; she's a big fan of journaling as a way to resonate with one's spirit.

Write to your children often, especially when teens. It keeps the lines of communication open. I used to leave little "I love you" notes in their pockets, a lunch box, a book, somewhere they might find it when I was not around. When my children were teens I wrote them letters and it was a way to get them to really *hear* what I had to say. It kept us close . I did not use the letters to berate them or to list their faults, but to encourage them, and let them know how important their choices were to me and the family.

JUDGING OTHERS: It is said when you point a finger at another, 3 fingers are pointing back at you. Interestingly enough, is the theory that what we judge in another is a mirror, what we do not like in them, we are also guilty of. There is a Native American proverb that says: "Don't judge another until you have walked a mile in his moccasins". This simply means if you were given the entire set of circumstances the person you are criticizing had to deal with in their lives, you probably would do the exact same things, might look the same way, etc., think about that, and judge less. The only ones we have a right to judge is ourselves, and often we do that too harshly. We are not born with judgmental attitudes but our homes and relatives teach us how to judge others and our childhood peers can encourage us to be harshly critical of others, something that might last a lifetime if we allow it to.

In the cycle of reincarnation, it is said that we ALL face the same challenges, only at different times. Those who judge a drug addict, and think, "I would NEVER do that," probably faced that test in a previous lifetime and should just be thankful they passed the test and do not have the desire to abuse a substance. Most addictions are born of pain and anxiety with the desire to escape. See Chapters P—Prejudice, R—Reincarnation.

CHAPTER K

Karma/Dharma, Kindness

KARMA: Karma and Dharma are related cycles. I think of it as the batteries that charge a life. Just as in our car battery, one pole is positive (Dharma) and its polar opposite (Karma) the negative. These two charge all of our activities, directions, missions, and the paths we choose in our Soul Contracts before conception. Hindu's call Karma "the wheel of balance." There is personal and universal Karma. It is cause and reaction. I have a friend who calls Karma "Captain Karma," That is the stern taskmaster who says: okay, you did this, it caused a reaction and here is a good swift kick to get you going in the right direction. The other theory is that if at some point in the soul's history, one handled a situation poorly, or angrily without concern for another, they will now experience the situation again. Once we *get* the lesson, AND get it right, we won't be re-tested. What are the lessons one might wonder?

Honor and Respect your Deity, and your Elders; don't lie, cheat or steal; don't be jealous or angry. Don't take someone else's man or woman. Don't murder or otherwise inflict harm (that includes yourself).

If you run into a fool and must defend yourself or in the case of military personnel, accept that killing is a must, or be killed. What "do not kill" means, is don't go out there and kill innocent people for no reason except you might not have a grip. In the case of suicide, many of us have had a loved one die by their own hand. They either were mentally ill or they just could see no other way out of their pain, or messes and thought hard times last forever.

I do NOT believe those souls don't go to heaven. Our Creator turns his back on no one. A Professor of Philosophy at UWM, Milwaukee, Wisconsin, said in his class that suicide "is the worst assault on other people". I do not believe that those who commit suicide think they are harming their loved ones. They might feel that they are doing them a favor but that is not the truth. Loved ones will feel guilty about what they did or didn't do; don't leave that legacy to your loved ones. I think most of us might get at least one suicidal thought in our lifetime, I do not believe that is "abnormal" but a karmic test to stay in the world and be strong; don't flunk it.

When we don't get a lesson right, the names and faces can change but the circumstances will repeat until we get it. Once we do get it, we are never challenged with that lesson again. That's the good news!

DHARMA: All of humanity is moving towards a major awakening and change in consciousness. Get on the web and research what the Mystics are saying, in their discourses on the changes. Dharma is the good that you do; when and how it comes back to you, sometimes many years later. It is the golden threads that are placed in your Spiritual Bank Account. It is walking a Sacred and Divine Path resonating with your Deity or Creator to the 7 rays of light; that part of you that is an Angel in Training.

This is an exciting time! It takes 12,000 Earth years to create and cause cycles of human change. Gosh! Are we ever ready! It takes 7 years to move through a Karmic cycle. Does that sound long? Look how far you have come in the past 7 years. Don't forget to work with the 7 main Chakras, get them clear and moving in the right direction. See Chapter C—Chakras

KINDNESS: We hear a lot about practicing random acts of kindness, an awesome practice that blesses everyone concerned. If you'd like to start a practice of your own and don't have a clue where to start, visit: http://www.actsofkindness.org/index.asp

Treating others with kindness, love and compassion is never a wasted effort. Even if it appears the kindness is mistaken for weakness; you are building blessings in your spiritual bank account that will return to you with interest, often when you least expect it or really need it yourself.

Kindness is a choice that often has a ripple effect and spreads far beyond what you do today. The world is very much in need of more kindness and little children should be taught this virtue early on since children can be very cruel, mimicking the adults who taught them to be critical.

CHAPTER L

Labor, Laughter, Letting go, Liars and Lies, Life, Lifemate, Light, Light Worker, Living, Loneliness, Love.

LABOR: We can consider our close personal relationships to be a "labor of love." The old saying: "A woman's work is never done," is very true today as it was in years gone by. As a woman I believe that we actually are the backbones of the family and relationships, although often, we don't get enough credit for our efforts.

The hardest physical labor you will ever do? Why, having a baby of course! After that, almost anything is a piece of cake.

LAUGHTER: Laughter is the best medicine! Ever notice a person who has a wonderful laugh? My daughter has one, and it is the sort that is almost magical. You have to smile with her. Practice a deep *belly laugh* and notice how good that feels. Make a decision to smile more, laugh more, and you will see a big difference in the people around you. Smiling has been documented to release *happy* endorphins in our brain.

LETTING GO: Letting go is a challenge, especially if we do not really want to or are afraid that if we let go of one person, that no one else will be there or will come into our life. Sometimes we have to let go of the old so that the new can find its way into our life. Older ladies used to say, "A new man can't come in if the old one is blocking the door." At times, we find ourselves going beyond letting go and we find we must banish someone from our life circle, or as the French would say: bid them adieu!

Many of us have heard: "If you love someone, set them

free..." But goodness, how do we set someone free when we don't want to let them go? While it is important to have faith in the love for someone special it is even more important to have faith in you, and to love yourself. To constantly dwell on the absence of another only serves to take away your clarity, focus and joy, in the right now.

We do not want to admit that we were wrong about someone or chose the wrong person to love. Do not let shame cause you to suffer alone. So what if you have to admit that you made a mistake? We come into this world to learn. We are all human and human beings make mistakes. The person who seeks help in spite of embarrassment at admitting what is going on in their life, is the person who will move forward to a vibrantly healthy, and happy life experience.

For me, it helped me to realize that I am a Spiritual Being having a Human Experience; many people come into and go out of our life; not all stay for a lifetime. See Chapters B—Banish, S—Soulmate.

LIARS AND LIES: Too often children are taught in the home to lie to others. How? You might wonder, Parents have been known to tell their children to answer the phone and say: "She or He isn't here." We call things like that "little white lies," or "fibs." The truth is, they are lies.

Some people just seem to have more of a natural ability to lie to themselves or others. The truth usually comes out in the end, and lies are hard to keep track of. Honesty in all that you say and do is the best policy. It isn't true that you can look at every person and tell when they are lying, some people you can. Others are very good at it and until you find out the truth later, you will not know they are lying. My Grandmother used to say: "It all comes out in the wash," and "a liar is a thief"; I have found in many cases that was true. See Chapter E—Ethics.

LIFE: Life is a classroom for the soul. Not everything and everyone in life will hurt you. I have heard: "the world is a stage," so choose your role and play it to the best of your ability. It is imperative that we remember, no matter how many times we have been hurt, that there ARE good people in the world.

"Life is what you make it". I've also heard this saying and didn't much like it! I found though that if you make good choices for yourself, life is a lot better and as you get older you will find that you are more comfortable within yourself. It is such a good feeling to be proud of what you have accomplished. It is important that we do pat ourselves on the back when we know we've done a good job or met a responsibility we found hard to do. Life is a gift, what you do with it is your gift back. Taking care of each other and our planet will cause beauty and joy to flow and we can live in peace. Remember, life is not measured by the number of breaths we take, but by the **moments that take our breath away**.

LIFEMATE: This is the person we spend our lives with. Soulmate? Of course, but we do have many soulmates in life, and we can't possibly marry all of them! Fortunate are those who have a mate who is loving, kind and stable; unfortunate are those who suffer with a less than desirable partner (often chosen through loneliness) and who stay with them for the rest of their lives. Barbara De Angelis Ph.D wrote an excellent book entitled: Are You The One For Me, I think it should be required reading in high school. Choose wisely Dear One when it comes to a mate, you might be with them for the rest of your life, not only that, but your children will have to live with them too.

LIGHT:

When your world is rocking and you feel fright,
Surround yourself in a circle of Golden/White light.
This is your protection either day or night.
Light will always penetrate the darkness, that's right!
I saw a glimpse of the heavens, never thought one might...
Until a Near Death Experience granted me the sight.
Heaven is a real place bathed in glorious light,
Souls there are gentle, as a feather floating out of sight.
We each have a job to do in the world that requires might
So everyday, encircle yourself in Golden/White light.
Your own light will grow and shine very bright,
As you elevate yourself, take the hand of a friend and hold on tight.

Each person you meet will benefit if you are walking in the light.

Each path you cross will be better for meeting a laser beam that's right!

LIGHT WORKER: If we are Spiritually awake we spend a good deal of time in mediation and light, and teach what we learn to others, and voila! We are a Light Worker.

Do not be afraid to search out the many spiritual paths available, some with roots in ancient times, some a bit newer. You will know you have found the right one when you feel that you are a good role model. You may spend a short or great deal of time in one study; but do not be afraid to continue looking; we grow in light by various and eclectic study.

The congregational religious services can serve to refuel your spirit. If you are in need of a spiritual refuel, go quickly to the nearest worship service; visit several until you feel like a connection has been made; then go often to life your spirit.

LIVING: The gift of life is a beautiful thing, a gift from a loving Creator. What we do with it and how we live, is our gift back. Living in this fast paced world will not always feel too easy. We have the stresses of working and bills, but that does not mean we cannot be happy while we are meeting our obligations.

LONELINESS: If you are lonely most of the time, chances are you are uncomfortable with yourself. Become your own best friend, you will feel less lonely. We do need people and there are good people in the world, so don't shut yourself off from others. See Chapter S—Self Esteem.

LOVE: Love is the most important lesson we come here to learn. Along the way, we might meet some Fools, Punks, Skunks or Drunks and we learn about making good choices for ourselves. We are in control of who we choose for a partner. Too often, we either give up control of our lives out of need, loneliness, or a seeming inability to run our own life and we think that is love. That isn't, that is fear which puts a damper on love.

"Do you know that most things in life are a decision?

Love, while it may be an emotion it is also a decision. Any relationship, even the most romantic and 'in love' relationship still depends upon the couple deciding to love, to respect, to honor, to cherish....not just when it is easy, but when the going gets tough. A decision that supports the emotion." Julia Havey

It is true that if you don't love yourself enough, you won't be able to properly love anyone else. Too often, we get love and lust confused. It is important to ask ourselves at the very beginning of a relationship, am I in love? Or, am I in lust? Give yourself time to let the relationship develop (like a fine wine) before declaring your undying love. I have seen too many people meet someone and declare they are in love quicker than they choose an outfit for an important event; I often tell clients: "hang onto your heart until your head knows what is going on".

Love soothes the soul, and brings out the best in others. Whether that be in humans, animals or plants; love doesn't attempt to control but nurtures the recipient. The best love around is one that is unconditional and genuine.

"Touch my mind and I will think of you, but touch my heart and I will never forget you," author unknown. Men and women do love each other, but it does seem to me that we love a bit differently; often women ask: "does he love me as much as I love him?" I think that woman seem to love more deeply due to their nurturing genes. That is not to say that men cannot nurture (they can) but women are more emotional (heart space) men are more mental (head space) so there is a difference in how we feel and respond. See Chapter S — Self Esteem.

CHAPTER M

Marriage, Maturing, Metaphysics, Meditation, Men, Menopause, Mind, Ministry, Miracles, Motherhood, Morals, Mouth, Music

MARRIAGE: A Sacred Union between two people who agree to be partners. Shop wisely for the person you will marry; don't let loneliness choose that partner for you, or be so in a hurry to be married that you do not take the time to choose the right partner. The more successful marriages are those who hold hands at 60 like they did at 16; those who make the time each week for a date night (no children, friends or acquaintances invited). Learning to become good life partners is a process, some of us get better at it as we go along; others never learn and wind up lonely.

That brings to mind a few rules for choosing a relationship.

1) Do not let your loneliness choose your relationships and do not rush into a marriage or relationship to escape a harsh home life

2) Do not get into a serious relationship with someone until the one you are currently in is over; give yourself time to get to know "you", who you are now, today, (relationships do change us for better or worse), before tying your life up with someone new.

3) Take time to get to know the person and family you are committing your life to.

MATURING: I told my children when they were teens, "growing up is the hardest thing you have to do in life." What I didn't realize at the time is that as long as we are breathing, we never stop growing!

According to Astrology we do not become adults until we are between the ages of 28—31, when we have our First Saturn Return. We take off our childhood garments, and wear the cloak of adulthood. Every now and then, a few of us miss something of maturity; its tough to run into an immature 40 year old! See Chapter A—Astrology.

METAPHYSICS: It means, "beyond the physical," and traditionally refers to philosophy, attempting to understand the basic nature of all reality; things seen or unseen, divine or human. The sciences of Astrology, Dowsing, Numerology, Tarot, and several others used to be known as "occult" studies; what a scary word! The are now called Metaphysical Studies, which has a definitely better tone and vibration.

The study of any branch of Metaphysics is lifelong study and will take you "beyond the physical" to study and understanding the Spiritual Realm and will awaken psychic ability. We have heard for a long time "we are all psychic", that is the truth even if we do not acknowledge that we are psychic; many people freely admit to having a "good intuition" and we've all heard of "women's intuition". Do not be afraid to study a branch of Metaphysics, you might become very wise! Personally, I believe the study of Numerology is the easiest concept to grasp and it is quite amazing to see how our entire name carries the vibration of a certain number.

MEDITATION: Prayer is when we speak, Meditation is when we listen. The first step to learning how to meditate, is to learn how to "quiet the mind," Once you have learned to quiet your mind long enough to meditate, explore some of the video tapes that show you how to meditate. See Chapter G—Grounding.

MEMORIES: Good memories are one of the spices of life and will bring a smile and a good feeling when they come to mind. Our minds are like a wondrous computer and we store memories, good or bad that pop up at anytime. Early memories can effect how we view the world and the people in it even to the end of our lives.

The not so good memories will give us flashbacks, when it is from severe trauma and left untreated can lead to post traumatic stress syndrome which can be crippling. A mental health professional can bring you to recovery, do not be afraid to seek out help- See also Chapter F—Forgiveness.

MEN: There are many good, honest, caring men in the world, wondrous souls who take good care of themselves, their families and communities.

We have to beware of the fools, punks, drunks and skunks who are also out there. They are the ones who will use and abuse you, manipulate you through sex or try to raise you after you leave your parents. If a man is a drinker or drug user, you can bet he will share his poisons with you; why? because then you can't complain about him, and in the case of drugs, if you get hooked, he's got an accomplice that will help him do nearly anything to get the drug of choice and finally, if you are *high* you can be easily manipulated to do his bidding, or to give him your money.

Too often, we don't want to be alone, so we take the first one that comes along, (sometimes without checking to see if they are worth keeping) and get ourselves into a whole peck of trouble. The man you just met might truly be MR. WONDERFUL, but, if you declare your undying love, before you really know him, you might find, that you've declared your love to someone who turns out to be "your worst nightmare." Choose wisely darlings, for you have to live with your choices.

Pay particular attention to how the men you meet talk about their moms. It gives a great clue as to how you will be treated later on. If they say that they "hate" their Mom, or didn't get along with her, most often, you are better off running in the other direction.

Communication in a relationship IS most important and something most of us don't learn until we are in a relationship and figure out that we aren't communicating well. Now we have Dr. Phil, check out his books, especially Relationship

Rescue if you have a troubling relationship. See Chapters C—Communication, S—Sex.

MENOPAUSE: A "rite of passage" in the female life cycle. On which often is looked at as a hindrance, but happy is the woman who discovers her own freedom through this cycle, in time to enjoy her life. It does not have to be the difficult time that we all have heard about, there is a lot of help available today. See Chapter H—Health.

MIND: Each individual mind is a unique production of eons of genetic and cultural evolution and personal history (upbringing, training, age). The computer has not yet been built that can top the capabilities of the human mind.

The care and keeping of the human mind is really quite simple even in our complex world. Clean living, good nutrients for the body, Bach Flower Remedies for the soul, and a commitment to develop a peaceful mind is really all it takes to form a positive mindset. If we are not taught about our sacred self, and live by self destructive tendencies we will develop a negative mind and thought process and do plenty of "stinkin thinkin", until we awaken to the fact that we want a better life and there are people who are living that experience.

Some of us have very busy minds indeed, quieting the "chatter and rapid thoughts can be quite a challenge. Grounding techniques can be of great help with that. Many people say they are unable to meditate because their "mind is too busy" and they don't know how to quiet it; grounding techniques are the answer! See Chapters G—Grounding, M—Mouth.

MINISTRY: You don't have to preach in a pulpit to have a ministry. Your life is a ministry, your work a ministry, your marriage, friendships, the raising of your children is a ministry. Being a good role model for others is something to strive for in every area of life and being a good role model is also a ministry!

I believe that our souls mission is to "go and preach to all nations" (Bible, Matthew 28:19). That does not mean build a church or go to foreign lands to preach, but how you communicate with your family, friends, children, spouse or coworkers. My interpretation is not that we preach with our words, but do so when we live as good role models in our everyday life, treating others with respect and love.

MIRACLES: I believe in miracles and see them often, right before my eyes; sometimes I shake my head, and look again :-) Do you believe in Miracles? If not, call your local Unity Church; usually they have a group that meets once a week or every month, called A Course In Miracles. That course is inexpensive, and worth the investment in your future, you can also find info online.

Angels love to assist in Miracles. Develop a personal relationship with Angels and you will be amazed at how everything comes together, when its threatening to fall apart. We are not meant to fail! See Chapter A – Angels.

MORALS: Many families teach their young good morals, then they go out into the world and find that many other people have no morals and they run into rough situations and people. Corruption has been around for generations in one form or another. Christians and other religions believe it is the work of satan, an evil influence geared to the downfall of humans.

Certainly much of society is preoccupied with sex and prostitution has been called "the oldest profession". Some married couples engage in open marriages and advocate what is known as "swinging". Some single couples are monogamous to one person while others date multiple partners simultaneously. Certainly we all have a sex drive that has to be managed.

The way we manage our sex drive is through making the choice to use morals. It is up to each of us to develop our own moral code and live by it. Until the world changes there will always be immoral people around; if you have a covenant or agreement with yourself to live by a high moral standard they will not be able to tempt you into actions that will leave you feeling degraded, unhappy and used.

MOTHERHOOD: I always felt that Motherhood was my greatest Blessing, but it does require a lot of WORK! It is a gift to be given another human life to guide. It can be a great challenge, if you haven't learned how to guide your own life properly. Most of us have our children and grow up with them. Whether you are a good mother or not, your children will never forget you, please be a good role model. It is said, and I believe that the prayers a mother prays for her child are among the strongest and most powerful. Don't forget to stop and play! Motherhood is forever, even when you and your adult child are good friends.

MOUTH: Some people seem to have an uncontrollable mouth. They open it and anything is liable to fall out! We have total control over what comes out of our mouth and it is up to us that what comes out of it is positive and uplifting to those around you. You often hear "If you don't have anything nice to say, don't say anything at all", and that is a good motto to live by. Discipline yourself to harm no one with the words of your mouth, in other words, if you are going to say something nasty, learn to literally "Bite Your Tongue"!

Interestingly enough, the people with "potty mouths" usually have rotten teeth. Is it because they didn't learn proper dental hygiene, or could it be that their words, some very nasty, or, harsh cursing, is the cause of them losing their teeth? If a person cares little about their human brothers and sisters, chances are very high they do not care about themselves; although I have heard very well groomed, professional people cuss like "drunken sailors".

Children learn to cuss in the home, sometimes before they learn the alphabet; teenagers think its a "cool" thing to do and adults seem to like the shock value and think their cursing drives their point home. Not only does cursing place a curse upon situations or people, (even animals are not immune) but it is very disrespectful. Until we learn to live and talk in a loving way, we will live in disharmony. See Chapters P—Patience, T—Tolerance.

MUSIC: Music can soothe the soul, find the kind that soothes your soul and lifts your spirit.

CHAPTER N

Nagging, Name Calling, Near Death Experience (NDE), Need, Niceness, Nurturing, Nutrition.

NAGGING: Years back the slang for wife was "the nag." The saying you "catch more flies with honey than you do with salt," is true. Learn to bite your tongue. Usually when someone nags a lot at someone else, they also whine. Isn't that a terrible duo? After time, other people will tune you out or simply leave you. Nagging and yelling seem to go hand in hand. Learn to develop good communication skills and teach yourself to respect other people as well as yourself. See Chapters A—Attitude, P—Patience, T—Tolerance.

NAME CALLING: Name-calling is a terrible thing that many people in the world engage in. It is the beginning of all other forms of abuse in society; children MUST BE TAUGHT BY EXAMPLE, not to call others names; if you call them names they will learn from you how to call others names; later on, they will call you names. In many of families, especially dysfunctional ones, name calling is a way of life.

Condoning name calling, even moderate seeming names, like "stupid" or "dumb" is harmful to everyone in the family. We can make the choice to not call others anything but their given names, or better yet, use the terms of endearment, almost everyone likes to be called sweetheart, or honey. There will be many happy people growing up if that choice is made. Someone said: "People will not remember what you do, but they will remember what you say." I remember the quote because it touched my own heart and life, but I do not remember the author. It is the truth. If you say hurtful things to another, that tape will replay over and over to them, until they decide to teach themselves to play new, positive tapes.

NEAR DEATH EXPERIENCE: Also known as **NDE.** There really is another world, the Spiritual Realm, beside this one. *I saw it with my own eyes* when I "died" on the operating table at age 25. Many people have had a Near Death Experience, and have written about them. Read "Embraced by The Light" by Betty J. Eadie. Pay attention darlings, it IS NOT "all over" when we die, our soul goes on. Heaven is a glorious and very busy place!

NEED: We all have needs there is no doubt about it. Just don't go overboard and become "needy" and dependent on others for your happiness, you will be disappointed every time. Remember you are a strong, vibrant, spiritual being having a human experience. Another can enhance our life, but if we need that person in order to be happy, we will find ourselves very unhappy if for some reason they are no longer there. Find the happiness within yourself and share it with the world, you will be loved.

NICENESS: A quality we strive for. Most toddlers are taught to "be nice"; it is the best way to get through situations and treat people. We get many opportunities to be nice, even when we fail miserably at it. Don't expect yourself to be perfect, but do, be nice. I used to tell my children: "If you don't have anything nice to say, don't say anything at all", now I am teaching that to my grandchildren. How I wish this would spread in the world. See Chapter T—Tolerance.

NURTURING: Women have nurturing genes, no doubt about it. However, when the woman isn't feeding her soul, through spirituality, the whole process can run amuck, and she can wind up being the worst abuser, often, in the name of "love." Training others is an act of love, but we must do it kindly. No one will do what you want them to do all of the time. If they do it 50% of the time, consider yourself blessed and give them a break.

Bless those nurturing genes, they take care of the world, and bless yourself for the woman you are. See Chapter L—Love.

NUTRITION: Many of us learn our nutritional habits as young children. If you live in a health conscious home you will be blessed with good nutritional habits, if not, you will have to teach yourself. There are many great nutrition books on the market today, find one that speaks to you and implement health conscious changes for your life before you get a major wake up call from illness. You have to want to do this, if you do not, go quickly to Chapter S—Self Esteem.

CHAPTER O

Obstetrician, Other Worlds, Overweight

OBSTETRICIAN: Most are wonderfully kind, caring souls. Many are good looking, best not to fall in love with yours; although it is normal, especially if you are having a difficult pregnancy or love life. The hardest doctor visits we make are to our OB/GYN doctors, because of the sensitive nature of these visits, I was especially happy to find a woman doctor that I love :-) That is not to berate the many wonderful male doctors who specialize in this area.

OTHER WORLDS: Amazingly, we can have a poor person living in a run down house, and within 10 miles, a wealthy person living the "good life." If those aren't two different worlds nothing is.

There really is another world, the Spiritual Realm, beside this one. Pay attention darlings, it IS NOT "all over" when we die, our soul goes on.

Most of us have read reports on Aliens, and Crop Circles, so the concept of Other Worlds is one we should become familiar with. See Chapter N—Near Death Experience.

OVERWEIGHT: I have never cared for the word "obesity" to me, that sounds awful. If you would like to do something about your weight, take up yoga, which helps integrate mind, body and spirit; join a water aerobics class, you will be amazed at how easily you can move in the water; just don't feel so *light* you over do in the beginning. If you feel too overweight to get to a gym, purchase an exercise video that appeals to you and work out at home until you feel comfy going to a club. You will be completely amazed at how the body responds to working out, pounds and inches can and will drop off.

There are three motivational websites that I visit often, Oprah, Dr. Phil, and Julia Harvey. Find one that feels right to you, visit often and stay motivated. Anyone can lose weight if we put our mind to it and have the support of others. Remember: "A moment on the lips, a lifetime on the hips!".

CHAPTER P

Pain, **P**arenting, **P**arents, **P**ath, **P**atience, **P**ersonal **P**ower, **P**ills, **P**lan your future, **P**ost Partem Depression, **P**rayers of a Mother, **P**rayers of Protection, **P**rayer to St. Michael, **P**rejudice, **P**ride, **P**rosperity, **P**rotection, **P**sychic Ability, **P**urpose

PAIN: When you are in physical or emotional pain, the affirmation: "I AM pure Spirit, and Spirit can feel no pain" is an excellent affirmation to use. It will help you cope. When you feel emotional pain and cannot seem to get past it, seek help, there is no stigma in seeking therapy. As the seriously ill person can tell you, there is nothing worse than constant physical pain; many people in emotional pain do not realize that therapy can really benefit them, but it can. If you visit one counselor and that didn't work out for you, seek out another until you find the one you really click with. We are not meant to suffer and we are not programmed to fail.

PARENTING: There are many good books out today on parenting, and great baby and child care books available. Children do not come with a set of instructions (Unless one is, or knows of a good Astrologer). A good book will give you a point of reference to start with. Yes, you will make mistakes, and yes, you will grow with your children. The children will love you unconditionally for their entire lives if you are a good parent! That is worth doing your best for, isn't it? Every child needs and deserves good parents. The most important thing to remember is to set a good example. Children learn by what you do, not by what you tell them to do. Becoming a good role model for them, winds up helping you too! Astrology can help you to know and understand your child or children in a way nothing else does.

You are never sure of how good a job you've done, until they grow up. That doesn't mean feel guilty if they make the wrong choices for themselves. Children have their own learning experience and life path as do all of us. The teenage years don't count in that measure, since they are still finding themselves and it is up to us to guide them to be their best and we are responsible for them until they reach age 18. Too much freedom too early will not help them and can hurt them terribly.

While it is good to be friends with your children, do not set out to be their friend, you are their parent and that must come first. See Chapters A—Astrology, S—Single Parenting.

PARENTS: One of life's greatest blessings is to have two parents who love each other and to be born into a family of loving people. There is an Native American phrase "It takes a whole village to raise a child", that makes a lot of sense to me. Happy people are nurturing and loving and it is uplifting to spend time with them. Parents who are committed to being good role models know the truth of "children learn by what they see not by what you say". Birth is a great miracle of life and human beings forever remember their parents.

Many people did not start out blessed with two loving parents who nurtured them from infancy to adulthood in a HEALTHY way. Some were born into "dysfunction junction" and experienced a lot of abuse growing up. No matter how severe the abuse young children will make many attempts to be close to and they will love their parent. If the childhood was one of drama and trauma there will be wounds to heal from. Being aware that there can be wounds gives us a place to start. We have to become our own loving parent, or our own best friend. We have to really care about what we put into our bodies and not do things we know are self destructive. We must learn to counteract negative "tapes" (memories we have or negative ways we were taught), with positive, loving and stable thoughts of self worth. Forgiveness is the bottom line to moving toward a happy life. See Chapters A—Abuse; I—F—Forgiveness; I—Inner Child, S—Self Esteem.

PATH: People change everyday until they find their own way. Our local Unity Church of Christianity has a billboard that read "One God many Paths", you can insert the name of the diety of your belief for God, but the point is, we have one Creator but many paths lead there. How we find our way to that Creator is up to us, but never be afraid to search.

There are a million or more paths one can follow to living a fulfilled and happy life; first you must know what your core values are. That is a matter of sitting down with yourself and listing the values you were raised with and what others you might like to adopt.

If you are confused about career choices, most cities have technical colleges that offer testing to help you figure out the fields your abilities and interests are compatible with.

If you feel the path you are on is destructive to you, get off it and choose another that's where free will comes in. We have free will to choose what to do or where to go and hopefully the sense to know when we are going in the wrong direction.

PATIENCE: We hear about it constantly and we all need it in daily living. Patience is not something we are born with; but we can teach ourselves to have and use it. Having patience is a process we grow into, the more we work at it, the more we have available to us. Life will also teach us patience as every decade brings a "test of patience" and many opportunities to grow in patience.

PERSONAL POWER: Some of us are just born timid, or shy; some of us were not taught well enough how to be happy and emotionally healthy individuals. If our early caretakers were very controlling or abusive we will feel that we are not able to take care of ourselves and easily "give our power away" to another controlling person.

We are Divine, Powerful beings of light; our light is the essence of who we are, also called soul. You might be thinking, who me? I have no power; well I say "that isn't so," you have it all right, you just don't know that you do! Awareness is what allows us to right ourselves. When we learn how to ground and center ourselves, all else flows, and that includes personal power. See Chapter D—Divine Self.

PILLS: Our Society leans towards the concept: "take a pill and fix it!" For some physical conditions that holds true. For emotional upheavals or some depression, a pill will not do it alone. I believe that too many doctors freely prescribe anti-depressants or tranquilizers without requiring the patient to get therapy help, either counseling or group therapy or both. I believe there should be a "marriage" of sorts and the two should go hand in hand; you are prescribed anti-depressants, and HAVE to get counseling to get at the real root of the problem. There really isn't a magic pill for life.

A well known addiction is to pain pills; yes of course we can and do have pain in our physical bodies from one reason or another, however, taking a pain pill will mask the problem, but won't make it better until we do whatever it takes to solve the problem. Please understand, I am NOT talking about serious illness; If you have chronic pain, get to the cause of what is wrong; consult with a pain clinic; do not be afraid to search out alternative or complimentary forms of healing; consult a chiropractor; learn of other healing modalities such as Acupressure, Acupuncture, Emotional Freedom Technique, Healing Touch, Reflexology, Reiki, there are many; find one that appeals to you and take responsibility to live the best PAIN FREE life you can. You can save a lot of money by working on the inner self instead of paying for prescriptions to mask the pain of it all.

PLAN YOUR FUTURE: We all have dreams of what we want to do, how and where we will live, etc. Sometimes our dreams are put on hold, but we can always go back, dust them off, and set goals. Education is the single best investment we can make for our life. I have heard and believe it to be the key to freedom.

No matter how far we have strayed from our dreams, it is never too late to accomplish what we decide we want to do. If you have no clue as to what you might be good at, most community colleges offer testing for free or nominal costs, check out the one in your area.

Sometimes events happen that take us in a different direction, that does not mean you cannot accomplish what you would like to. The rule of thumb today is simple: Believe it, Achieve it! See Chapter A—Achieving Goals.

POST PARTEM DEPRESSION: This can be a very real, traumatic time; I believe has roots in the drop in hormones the body produced during pregnancy. Depending on the life circumstances, and the emotional makeup of the new mother, this can be barely noticeable, or a very challenging time.

Nothing is more beautiful than a mother with her newborn, but that picture can have a very real traumatic side also; I personally believe that all newborns are beautiful but I've heard new mothers say, "oh he looks like an ugly old man". She didn't know she would melt the first time he smiled at her. Does that mean you will automatically love your child the moment you see him or her? well, not always; it is an major adjustment; what if you don't feel instant love? Just be gentle with yourself and give yourself time to grow into your new role. It can be downright scary; you are now responsible for a tiny creature who cannot tell you what is wrong or why they are crying. That alone can drive a person to despair.

Adding to the mix is the fact that you are now getting up every couple of hours, tending to the baby and if there are other children there are more demands at a time when you feel like you just were ran over by a truck; the more support you have the better, for this time does not last forever and will pass. I found girlfriends to be a big help, even more than family, although well meaning, everyone wants to give you tips on how to raise baby. Trust your own instincts.

If your life is more stable, and you are a very spiritual person, you will flow through this time, with perhaps a few tearful moments. If you have a colicky baby, or several other children and not too much help while recovering, or have financial problems, this can be a challenge and seemingly awful time in the life. Note: I did not say fatal!

Do one nice thing for yourself and know this time, too, shall pass. Seek professional help so that you continue to enjoy your life and the new little person entrusted to your care. Please do not be afraid to call your doctor if you are feeling down in the dumps; he or she will not think bad of you or that you are a terrible mother; doctors know this is common problem for new mothers, get the help you need to allow your body and mind the time you need to adjust to this life changing event.

PRAYERS OF A MOTHER: The prayers of a Mother for her child are among the strongest known. Pray for your children on a daily basis. Use the Prayer of Protection around them and all you love. Take the few extra minutes to encircle each of your children individually, don't just say "around my children.

PRAYERS OF PROTECTION: The Prayer of Protection I was fortunate enough to learn when my twins were approximately two years old, and has never been know to fail when invoked:

The Prayer goes like this:
By the Name and in the Power of the Living Christ,
I take upon myself
(car, home, loved ones, strangers in trouble)
A wall of living flame of protection
(at this time actually picture a circle
going completely around you
or the object needing protection).
I give thanks that it is done,
It Is done, IT IS DONE!
(Metaphysical Law of 3)
and I am grateful!
Source unknown.

There is also a "long form" of the Prayer of Protection (in the Bible), it is very powerful can be used for meditation, protection or just to pray. As you recite this do not just say the words, actually picture these directives as you say them:

By the Name and in the Power of the Living Christ,
I take upon myself: The whole Armor of God.
I wear the Helmet of Wisdom,

The Breastplate of Honor,
My feet are shod in Peace,
My loins are girded in Truth,
On my left arm is the Band of Salvation,
In my right hand is the Double-edged Sword
of the Holy Spirit.
Heavenly Father, Let Thy Holy Spirit
Descend and Infill me now, that whatever
shall come by way shall be Truth and Peace
and only that.
It is Done, It is Done, IT IS DONE.
I am Grateful

Once you are covered by the Circle of Protection, imagine yourself with mirrors all around you; These mirrors, deflect, and reflect any negativity sent your way, back to the source sending it, with love.

Important to note is that it will last approximately four hours and then needs to be said again. The reason for that is the amount of negativity that is present in the world. I try to be careful not to be a part of any negative energy or conversations.

PRAYER TO ST. MICHAEL:

Saint Michael the Guardian Angel, defend us in battle. Be our protection against the wickedness and snares of the devil; May God Rebuke him we humbly pray, and do Thou, Oh Prince of the Heavenly Host cast into hell Satan and all evil spirits who wander throughout the world seeking the ruin or discomfort of souls. Amen.

PREJUDICE: Prejudice is rampant in the world. A preconceived notion sometimes handed down from one generation to another that one race or culture is better than another; or one of anything is better than another, or, the only way.

Prejudicial type feelings are very harmful to human race as a whole. We all bleed red blood, the only real differences being if we are born with male or female equipment, language, how we are trained by our family or culture. It never ceases to amaze me how one minority will consider themselves to be better than another race. We are all One! We are part of the human family.

PRIDE: Taking pride in one's Country, family and the self is a very good thing. It is so much better to have that type of pride than to beat yourself up for everything that seems wrong or to be too critical. There is a special glow to parents who are proud of themselves and their children.

False pride is the brand of pride which is compounded of the vanity and ill-nature that compels men to admire themselves and condemn others. "Pride can be as loud a beggar as want, and a good deal more impudent. When we have acquired one fine piece of raiment, we immediately rush to buy a dozen more, so that our appearance may be suitably matched. It is far easier to suppress the first desire than to satisfy all that will follow," Ben Franklin.

PROSPERITY: Understanding that prosperity is a blessing, and treat it accordingly, causes more blessings to be given to you. Money begets money, you've often heard that said. It is the truth. We are not meant to "worship" money, but to enjoy the comfort that money can add to the life. Bless what you do have and it will increase; don't pronounce yourself "broke," something that is broke cannot be fixed. We live in an abundant Universe with enough of everything for everyone!

Affirmations of all kinds are available to us to help us raise our vibration from lack and despair to love and light. The more we discipline ourselves to drill in positive affirmations, the more we keep negativity at bay. To walk a path of Light and Love is to know complete joy in the here and now. This is not to say that you might not get a flat tire from time to time, but when you do, look for the good in the situation. The kind help you received, a ride home, an understanding officer; even if you had no spare, look for the good. Do not let the flat (or other situation) upset you to the point that all you can do is think about the experience in terms of how unlucky you are or how stressful it was.

From Erma Bombeck's books I learned the necessity of always having a plan, in fact two of them, Plan A and Plan B and be able to switch from Plan A (what you thought) to Plan B (what you got) without getting upset and ruining the whole day. Remember that "Anger is one letter away from Danger", when operating from an angry space, anything can happen.

If money is tight, your life isn't working to the best it can be and you don't have a plan. Without a vision or a plan, circumstances seem to take over and we can become lost in them and afraid. Fear is the absence of faith, a necessary ingredient to a peaceful and prosperous life. Every New Year we wish each other A Happy and Prosperous New Year; we hear the word "prosperous" and we think: Oh, I hope so! Choose to believe that it IS so.

You have nothing to lose and everything to gain by adopting a prosperous attitude. Keep a journal for the next 30 days and list what blessings come your way when you are doing prosperity affirmations. The neat thing is that when you affirm that "My life and affairs are in Divine Order", you life does actually feel like Divine Order is operating. Here is a series of affirmations that I love to use:

This is from a book written by a dear enlightened woman and minister who became my mentor while I was cutting my Metaphysical teeth. "It is Time For You To Be Financially Free" By Patricia Diane Cota-Robles

"My Life now reflects the Gift of Permanent Financial Freedom From this moment forth, everything I need to fulfill my Divine Plan is always available to me. The Divine Law of "Ask and you shall receive" is instantly manifest I feel the buoyancy and elation of my newfound freedom and the entire Company of Heaven rejoices with me as I reclaim my Divine Birthright of Abundance through Prosperity Consciousness.

* I AM! I AM! I AM! . The eternally sustained manifestation of God's limitless supply of Money and every Good thing I require to assist me in my service to the Light, now made manifest and sustained by Holy Grace (Repeat three times from * It is done! It is done! it IS done! and I AM grateful"

PRAYER FOR GRATITUDE AND ACCEPTANCE

"Through the Power of God anchored in my Heart and within the Hearts of ALL Humanity, I invoke the Divine Flames of Gratitude and Acceptance. Precious Sacred Fire, blaze in, through and around every electron of my Being. Flood my consciousness with Gratitude for and the acceptance of God's Limitless Flow of Abundance. Lift me into the Realms of Truth, and Bless me with the clear Inner Knowing that the God Supply of all good things is my Divine Birthright.

I relinquish now, in the Name of God, all of the power I have ever given to lack and limitation through my thoughts, words, actions or feelings.

I relinquish now, in the Name of God, all of the beliefs I have ever had that are based in poverty consciousness.

In deep Humility and Gratitude, I consecrate and dedicate my very life to be the open door through which God's Limitless Abundance will flow to Bless me, my family, friends, co-workers and ALL Humanity.

As I think, speak, feel and act, the Presence of God within me is expanding God's Gift of Prosperity to all life evolving on Earth.

I AM an Awakened Light Being! I Gratefully accept God's Gift of Prosperity and Limitless Abundance! And So It Is! I AM! I AM! I AM!"

Create a list of your own affirmations for abundance and prosperity, and get the blessings flowing into your life. Remember to say thank you, as gratitude keeps blessings flowing. Rev. Catherine Ponder has a wonderful series of prosperity books in print. See Chapter G—Gratitude.

PROTECTION: When we love ourselves, it is okay for us to protect ourselves. That does not mean be paranoid about your life, just look out for yourself, in other words, "watch your back". Make good choices of friends and good decisions for yourself.

Psychically we are like a sponge, hence the need for prayers of protection so that we do not "soak up" other people's energy when we come in contact with them. If we do and from time to time we will, pick up energy from other people, grounding and centering will help you to clear it out. We can stand next to someone in line or in an elevator and pick up energy from them. Often we shake hands and can pick up energy from another person. If we are very empathic (and many of us are) we will pick up energy from another from conversations, whether that be in person or via the telephone. See Chapter G—Grounding.

PSYCHIC ABILITY: Everyone has psychic ability, an inner knowing of what's coming or what to do next. Psychic ability takes on many forms, if you want to know more, just do a website search on Psychic Ability. Some people are born with the gift and know it from a very young age. Others have a life altering experience, often a Near Death Experience that opens psychic channels in an amazing way; still others study till they *get it*. Many people are afraid to see something coming that isn't pleasant, so they do not want to open psychic ability. I suggest to you that it is in seeing something unpleasant coming up that we can be a miracle in someone else's life. You might be wondering how that is, but the truth about it is that when I see something coming for someone, I begin to pray for and bless them or the situation I see coming. I have seen many times, what would be considered a miracle. Did I do that work in and of myself? No, I was merely the channel, Our Creator grants all miracles.

PURPOSE: "Each mans road is shown to him within his own heart. There he sees all the truth of life." Cheyenne teaching.

Many of us look for some major purpose to be revealed to us, as though we aren't living it every day, and it is something that will magically present itself to us one day in a moment of enlightenment. Our purpose is to be who we are, male or female, whatever race, daughter/son of someone, and related to others in the family. Friends come and go, although some of us are blessed with friendships that last the entire live. Life is a classroom for the soul, and our soul's purpose is to decide which path to take to live the most righteous life possible, then to commit to living it. Life has many lessons, and learning how to use our free will for the good of all is a major one.

"You can take life as it comes,
or you can grab it by the horns
ABC News Anchor

We have some rules, the 10 Commandments, and other

various cosmic and/or universal laws to follow. We can choose other creeds to live by, for instance, The Reiki Creed:

1. For today, I will be grateful for all things.
2. For today, I will not worry.
3. For today, I will not anger.
4. I will do my work honestly.
5. I will show love and respect to all living beings.

Accept yourself for who you are, that is a huge part of our life's purpose. Isn't that simple? To be who we are and doing our best to live a righteous life. Sometimes things are so simple we can miss them, looking for larger reasons that don't seem to come to us; or expect ourselves to wake up one day with the knowledge: "This Is Your Purpose!" If we think that, we can miss a lot of happiness in our lives. Cultivate the attitude that each individual is part of the Divine Plan and all are connected.

The next large part of our reason for existing is to make a choice as to what Spiritual Path we will follow, we have free will and can choose what we will believe. Choose only a path that will "DO NO HARM".

CHAPTER Q

Queen, Quiet Time, Quit

QUEEN: You are the QUEEN of your household! Remember that, and always act accordingly. Using harsh words, cursing, and general mean ways is not honoring yourself or others you live with. That includes plants and animals. I cannot say enough about honoring yourself for the woman you are. If you don't like who you are at the moment, honor the woman you would like to become. In other words: fake it, till you make it! See Chapter S—Self Esteem.

QUIET TIME: We all need quiet time. If you have a busy household, take the time for a bubble bath to get away by yourself for a few minutes and just relax. We all need quiet time to take inventory on where we are, to set goals, to meditate, or get in touch with your spirit. Arrange your schedule to allow for some quiet time at least three times a week, but preferably get in 30 minutes (at least) everyday. If you have an extra room in your home, make it a Meditation Room, a sacred space where you can just "be". See also Chapter S—Sacred Space.

QUIT: There are times when we should not quit just because the going might be tough. That is the time the tough get going. There are other times when we better know when to quit and go in a different direction.

Some things in life we had better quit! As soon as the small voice inside says "you better quit doing this", listen to it and get the help you need.

"Sometimes quitting is the right choice especially when you feel stuck in a comfortable but unfulfilling relationship or stay in a job that is not in alignment with your soul path and gifts. Why do most people quit? Fear of failure and often simple indecision. When we resist change the universe forces it and the effect is usually more difficult than change made voluntarily at the right time. So learn to go with the flow and do stay on task regardless of obstacles in the way of your dreams!" Suzann Ricky. See also Chapters A—Addiction, B—Banish, L—Letting go.

CHAPTER R

Rape, **R**eflexology, **R**eiki, **R**eincarnation, **R**elationships, **R**eligion, **R**espect, **R**isk, **R**ole model, **R**un-a-way

RAPE: A sexual violation with effects that can last a lifetime **if** one allows it to play over and over in the mind. Flashback memories can happen at anytime or place, with no warning and you could instantly relive the memory. Rape is an act by a sick individual. There are several forms of rape, date rape, violent rape in an ambush situation, or even the rape of a husband upon an unwilling wife; It is my opinion that rape upon an innocent child is the worst thing we can do to each other in this world!

The statistics are very high and the chances of experiencing at least one rape in your lifetime great. The first and foremost thing to remember is get yourself to a hospital for a rape test kit. There are by far more sensitive treatments available now than ever before. Most women feel shame and all they want to do is shower first. Please don't do that, seek help immediately.

I say, that rape doesn't have to be the end of the world, although we feel like it might be when it happens. Yes, it happens, but instead of thinking of yourself as a rape victim, call yourself a survivor, for that is truly what you are. The rape does not have to ruin your life. If you find yourself with an insensitive husband, let him become your "ex," and have a relationship with someone who respects you. That will go a long way towards you respecting yourself.

A rape does not mean you aren't a good person, or somehow asked for it, or brought it upon yourself. That is not the truth.

Don't let it be true for you. PS: Join a support group and if it is possible, press charges; be aware that professional therapy is extremely important at this time to avoid a condition known as Post Traumatic Stress Disorder.

There are women who have found themselves pregnant after a rape and decide to go through with the pregnancy. It is a special responsibility to stay conscious of the fact that a child conceived from a rape had nothing whatsoever to do with what happened to the mother. I personally knew a mother, who would quickly tell everyone she met (in front of the child) that he was conceived because of a rape. Saying such things can place a terrible burden on the child, please consider that.

See also Chapter A—Abortion.

REFLEXOLOGY: An ancient form of healing dating back to the Egyptians. Reflexology works with the nerve endings in the hands and feet. Most Reflexologers work with the feet, although the hands can also be reflexed quite well; we use our hands more, all day long, so the feet seem to take the treatment better.

I have done reflexology on newborns, so I know it *works* even right after birth. My daughter called me from the hospital in a panic and said: "Mom, the baby isn't able to suck right, they are going to put a tube down her throat if she doesn't start sucking." I said, okay, I'll be right there. I took those tiny little feet and rosebud toes, and did a complete reflexology treatment, paying particular attention to the throat area where I was surprised to find a rather large size lump (large for a tiny foot), I massaged the area and the lump out, 20 minutes later, the baby was sucking a bottle like she was supposed to!

REIKI: A Japanese modality of healing that means Universal Energy. Here is a good introduction: Reiki (pronounced Ray-Key) is a method of natural healing based on the application of Universal Life Force Energy (the name literally means Universal Life Force Energy). Reiki is one of the more widely known forms of healing through direct application of Chi, or a force very similar to Chi for it may be that Chi is different from the energy used by Reiki.

Chi is the term used by the Chinese mystics and martial artists for the underlying force the Universe is made of. Mystics in all cultures have talked about the physical universe being made of an underlying simpler form of something, much as modern physics research is now coming to understand that "something" is that the Universe is made of energy which is subject to (or affected by) thought. Just as modern physics says this energy is affected by thought the mystics also say this underlying form is affected by thought, going so far as to claim we create our own reality from our thinking and the thoughts we share between each of us every day. *(author/source unknown) If you wrote this or know who did, please email me so that I may give proper credit in future revisions of this work.

REINCARNATION: This is the belief that when one dies, the soul leaves the body, goes to heaven for a time, and then is reborn into another body. The theory of reincarnation began with the ancient Eastern religions like Hinduism and Buddhism but can now be found in Western New Age therapies such as past life regression therapy. The theories are that current life problems can be found in past lives or are karmic conditions. Edgar Cayce believed he was in touch with numerous of his past lives. It is certainly worth exploring for one's self. See Also Chapter k—Karma.

RELATIONSHIPS: We don't get to choose our family members but each one deserves love, care and respect, for the simple fact they are blood relatives. Relationships require taking a *Risk*, most are well worth the time and effort. I heard: "Relationships are 90% work, the other 10% we are sleeping"! That is pretty much the way it is. Relationships require unselfish giving and unconditional love if they are to stand the test of time. If you don't agree with someone, agree to disagree, but love them anyway.

Attempting to control another will put a huge dent in the relationship somewhere down the line and cause it to fall apart. Not everyone is going to do what you want or think is right MOST of the time. You cannot change another person, you can ONLY CHANGE YOURSELF. If you want change to happen in another person, change your attitude towards them and change those parts of yourself that might cause unhealthy reactions in someone you love.

If a relationship isn't feeling *right*, that is your intuition telling you to get out. It isn't the right relationship if you are unhappy, hurt, or feeling used. Trust your feelings on that. Do not let shame or pride, cause you to suffer alone. So what if you have to admit that you made the wrong choice in partners, we are all human and human beings make mistakes. I believe that the mistakes are actually *lessons* and we all get them in this classroom of Life.

We all can have the tendency to fall in love too quickly, it's easy, because being in love is a starry eyed, warm, fuzzy, feeling, and we LIKE being in love. Often we love our spouse or mate but are not in love with them. Take enough time to get to know the person. We can believe we love someone especially if we become intimate right away. That isn't love, its more like being in lust. We take more time shopping for clothes than we do for the right relationship, especially if we are letting loneliness choose for us.

RELAXATION: Many of us know intellectually that relaxation is important, yet often we are unable to relax in our busy world. There are many great self help books available on this topic. but first you have to become aware that you really do not know how to relax, in order to change. I believe that there are MANY souls in this world who cannot relax. In the case of those who received harsh caregiving as a child, they may not be aware that there are but a few times when they really feel relaxed. We can only fix what we acknowledge. Take a personal inventory of how often and when you really can say you relaxed. If you journal, make a note of whether or not you felt relaxed on the date of the entry.

You might ask yourself the following question: Am I happy? (if you are unhappy, I'd bet you seldom relax.

Grounding Techiniques can be a great help in learning how to relax. and release tension and stress. As mentioned there are great self help books available. If there are children in your life, get out and really play with them. You will relax (if not, you'll be tired enough to relax completely when the playtime is over). Find one thing daily to have a "belly laugh" over.

It is said prayer is when we speak and Meditation when we listen yet many people do not have a clue on how to meditate. or think it to be "weird" or "new age" and therefore reject this as something to learn. Find a meditation class in your area and learn this very important tool for relaxation. See Chapter—G—Grounding.

RELIGION: There are six major World Religions: Animism, Buddhism, Christianity, Hinduism, Islam and Judaism, with evidence dating back 100,000 years and continues to be very influential in today's living. It is my belief that following a religious path is of great help and comfort while facing life's challenges. There are numerous religions, while different, all serve the same purpose. Our local Unity Church (Unity School of Christianity) had a billboard which read: "Many paths, one God". If your life isn't working as well as you think it could, find your path to the Creator of all.

RESPECT: Some of us are taught to respect others from young on, others have to learn respect the hard way; they do not realize how much easier the life will flow if they treat everyone in their life circle with respect. We have a choice whether we want to live respectfully and respect others or let life happen to us. Dr. Philip MacGraw (Dr. Phil) says "we teach people how to treat us," if we treat them with respect, we teach others to respect us. See Also Chapter G—Golden Rule.

RISK: The following is a poem to live by, written by a colleague of mine. Love is a risk, as are all of our close relationships in the beginning. The *Risk* is well worth taking.

~ RISK ~

I spent my life never taking a single risk
and never taking a chance I spent it alone.
I spent my lifelike it was a box of coupons
going from store to store looking for the best deal
and I ended up paying full price anyway.
I spent my life waiting for the next bus

thinking that that one was the "express"
and I never got anywhere at all.
(I should have walked.)
I spent my life wanting...Something, ANYTHING!
and never risked a darn thing
Could that be why I didn't find what I was looking for?
Could that possibly be it?
I spent my life As if I had limited credit
...Next time—-I'm going to be a Platinum card
and spend it with STYLE.
NEXT TIME....I'm going to take risks
I'm going to celebrate
I'm going to live in the moment
WAIT! My life isn't OVER!
I don't have to wait for "next time"
I can do this NOW!
If I only had one week to live
...(and who knows how long I really have?)
Risks would come easily to me...
I could dance in the rain
I could wear funny clothes in public
I could kiss someone
and watch their face while I do!
I could be silly
I could be successful
I could be MORE than I have ever dreamed...
Yes, I could even dream again...
and live those dreams...
Living in this moment..
I can be someone who is fully absolutely ALIVE!
YES YES YES! That is the plan!
All I have to do...Is take off the safety shield
move out of the comfort zone
and take responsibility for my life....
ALL??? Gosh, a lifetime of programming...
Can I do it?
What the heck...I'm gonna give it my best shot.

And if I fail...I can celebrate that I tried. And I WILL! :)
And if I succeed!! !OH MY! What a feat!
THAT thought alone...is....
.Worth the RISK!
©1998 by Susan Holm

ROLE MODEL: No matter what our age, the world needs good role models, whether you are a child of 6 or a child at heart, of 60. Becoming a good role model for those in our life circle is a great decision and one that will bring respect many times over in our lives.

RUN-A-WAY: There are times we'd all like to run away, some of us act on it and can get in BIG trouble (especially if one is a teenager, since teens can be easily victimized). The most important thing to remember if you are considering running away, is that you cannot run away from yourself and you will take yourself with you.Better to stay and get professional therapy if you feel that your life is not going the way you want it to.

If you are a teenager, and are considering running away from home, or you are what is called a "throw-away", PLEASE seek help through a social service agency in your state. If you live in Wisconsin, there is a United Way Agency called Pathfinders for Runaways (serving ages 11-17) that is very good and they will help you before "the streets" swallow you up. **Pathfinders for Runaways** (A service of The Counseling Center of Milwaukee, Inc.)1614 East Kane Place, Milwaukee 53202 (414) 271-1560; FAX: (414) 271-1831; Email: pfjames@execpc.com or pflisa@execpc.com. See Chapter C—Crossroads.

CHAPTER S

Sacred Self, Sacred Space, Sacrifice, Safety Tips, Sage, Seasons, Self esteem, Self pity, Sex, Sincerity, Single living, Single parenting, Soul, Soul Contracts, Soulmates, Spirit, Spirituality, Spiritual living, Strength, Stress, Substance abuse, Suicide, Sun-charged Water, Surgery, Synchronicity

SACRED SELF: Once I got it out of my *head* (intellect) and into my heart (feeling) that I am a Spiritual Being having a Human experience, I began to look at life as more of an adventure. It has been said: "Life is a journey to be savored, not a race, to be won." The Sacred Self is that spark of the Divine that you are. If you don't feel connected to the Divine, start attending church, seek out a spiritual path that you feel a connection with and start reconnecting yourself to Spirit; just remember that the path you choose should "do no harm."

SACRED SPACE: Many people, including Joseph Campbell wrote of the need for a sacred space. He said, "You must have a room or a certain hour of the day or so where you do not know what is in the morning paper. A place where you can simply experience and bring forth what you are and what you might be. At first you may think nothing's happening. But if you have a sacred space and take advantage of it and use it everyday, something will happen".

You do not need a large space, it can be in your bedroom, an alcove, in the attic or basement, just an area you designate as your own sacred space. I prefer an area adorned with what I consider to be treasures (can be as simple as a rock from a special place), make it peaceful and beautiful. Happy are those people who consider their entire home to be a Sacred Space.

Spend time there as often as possible, whether in meditation, or just to contemplate and explore your creative energy. We must take the time to listen to our inner self, and a sacred space helps you to open to that hearing.

I believe that every home should have an altar with design and objects you consider sacred; it adds great energy to any room.

SACRIFICE: There are many times in life that sacrifice is required of us in one form or another. As a Christian, when I am faced with something that I don't particularily want or like to do, I offer it up as a sacrifice for Jesus Christ being nailed to the cross. There are times I willingly give a gift of time, or money as a random act of kindness and silently offer that up as well. It may not be necessary for one to think of sacrifice in these terms, but it sure helps me cope and maybe even smile as I am doing a difficult task! See Chapter K—Kindness.

SAFETY TIPS: Reminders to keep us around and safe. Please take the time to read this. I know you are smart enough to know these pointers but there will be some, where you will go "hmm, I must remember that."

THE TIPS:

1. Tip from Tae Kwon Do: The elbow is the strongest point on your body. If you are close enough to use it, do!

2. Learned this from a tourist guide to New Orleans. If a robber asks for your wallet and/or purse, DO NOT HAND IT TO HIM. Toss it away from you.... chances are that he is more interested in your wallet and/or purse than you and he will go for the wallet/purse. RUN LIKE MAD IN THE OTHER DIRECTION!

3. If you are ever thrown into the trunk of a car: Kick out the back tail lights and stick your arm out the hole and start waving like crazy. The driver won't see you but everybody else will. This has saved lives.

4. Women have a tendency to get into their cars after shopping, eating, working, etc., and just sit (doing their checkbook, or making a list, etc. DON'T DO THIS! The predator will be watching you, and this is the perfect opportunity for him to get in on the passenger side, put a gun to your head, and tell you where to go. AS SOON AS YOU GET INTO YOUR CAR, LOCK THE DOORS AND LEAVE.

5. A few notes about getting into your car in a parking lot, or parking garage:

A. Be aware: look around you, look into your car, at the passenger Side floor, and in the back seat.

B. If you are parked next to a big van, enter your car from the Passenger door. Most serial killers attack their victims by pulling them into their vans while the women are attempting to get into their cars.

C. Look at the car parked on the driver's side of your vehicle, and the passenger side. If a male is sitting alone in the seat nearest your car, you may want to walk back into the mall, or work, and get a guard/policeman to walk you back out. IT IS ALWAYS BETTER TO BE SAFE THAN SORRY.(And better paranoid than dead.).

6. ALWAYS take the elevator instead of the stairs.(Stairwells are horrible places to be alone and the perfect crime spot.).

7. If the predator has a gun and you are not under his control, ALWAYS RUN! The predator will only hit you (a running target) 4 in 100 times; and even then, it most likely WILL NOT be a vital organ. RUN!

8. As women, we are always trying to be sympathetic: STOP IT! It may get you raped, or killed. Ted Bundy, the serial killer, was a good-looking, well educated man, who ALWAYS played on the sympathies of unsuspecting women. He walked with a cane, or a limp, and often asked "for help" into his vehicle or with his vehicle, which is when he abducted his next victim. Author Unknown. While I cannot give credit to who wrote it, I APPLAUD their efforts to keep women safe but these rules can apply to all of us.

SAGE: This isn't about the variety of sage that you season a turkey with, this is about a bundled sage stick, a

Native American technique for dispelling negativity. *Smudge* yourself and your home. The smudging is done by moving the sage stick in a circular manner, around yourself; you might say nothing, or affirm: As of right now, all negativity within and without me is dispelled." You smudge your home by lighting the tip of the bundle and going from room to room, doing all of them; I usually affirm: "All negativity within and without this room is dispelled". Some smudge sticks are made with Sage and Sweetgrass, those work very well too.

SEASONS: There is a time to live, a time to die and a right time for everything in-between. Note that I did not say that it is in our time, because we want it right now. People come into our lives for a day, a season, or a lifetime, but always for a reason. Cherish your good memories, always be happy to go out and create more good memories. If you run into a few rough folks, hold onto the fact that there ARE good people in the world. Life is a journey for the soul.

SELF ESTEEM: We do the most harm to ourselves when we lack self-esteem. Didn't get it as a child? It is something you can teach yourself. All it takes is COMMITMENT to learning how to love yourself because you DESERVE to love yourself. If we don't love and respect ourselves, we cannot possibly expect anyone else to be able to love us. If self-esteem is damaged, it probably needs some work. Here is an exercise for self esteem.

Write out 2 copies of this, one to read daily; the other to cut into one liners and place all over, a purse, pocket, book, drawer, etc. When you come across one during the day, make yourself stop and really read it thru; After 90 days of this, your subconscious will supply an affirmation each time you are doubting yourself. Treat this work like a diet, if you skip a day, start over. It took me 2 years to do a solid 90 days of this work, but once I did, it changed my life forever, even to the point that I felt a weight had been lifted off my shoulders, (the "chip on my shoulder was gone?) it will change yours too. I received this in email many years ago, author/source unknown but it is worthy to be learned:

AFFIRMATIONS FOR SELF-ESTEEM

WHAT I AM:

I AM LOVABLE AND CAPABLE
I FULLY ACCEPT AND BELIEVE IN MYSELF
JUST THE WAY THAT I AM.
I AM A UNIQUE AND SPECIAL PERSON.
THERE IS NO ONE ELSE QUITE LIKE ME
IN THE ENTIRE WORLD.
I ACCEPT ALL THE DIFFERENT PARTS OF MYSELF.
I AM ALREADY WORTHY AS A PERSON.
I DON'T HAVE TO PROVE MYSELF
MY FEELINGS AND NEEDS ARE IMPORTANT.
IT'S OKAY TO THINK ABOUT WHAT I NEED
IT'S GOOD FOR ME TO TAKE TIME FOR MYSELF.
I HAVE MANY GOOD QUALITIES.
I BELIEVE IN MY CAPABILITIES AND VALUE
THE UNIQUE TALENTS I CAN OFFER THE WORLD.
I AM A PERSON OF HIGH INTEGRITY AND SINCERE
PURPOSE.
I TRUST IN MY ABILITY
TO SUCCEED AT MY GOALS.
I AM A VALUABLE AND IMPORTANT PERSON.
I AM WORTHY OF THE RESPECT OF OTHERS
OTHERS PERCEIVE ME AS A GOOD
AND LIKEABLE PERSON
WHEN OTHER PEOPLE REALLY GET TO KNOW ME,
THEY LIKE ME
OTHER PEOPLE LIKE TO BE AROUND ME
THEY LIKE TO HEAR WHAT I HAVE TO SAY
AND KNOW WHAT I THINK. OTHERS RECOGNIZE
THAT I HAVE A LOT TO OFFER
I DESERVE TO BE SUPPORTED BY
THOSE PEOPLE WHO CARE FOR ME
I DESERVE THE RESPECT OF OTHERS.
I TRUST AND RESPECT MYSELF
AND, HAVE THE RESPECT OF OTHERS.
I NOW RECEIVE ASSISTANCE AND

COOPERATION FROM OTHERS.
I AM OPTIMISTIC ABOUT LIFE.
I LOOK FORWARD TO AND ENJOY
NEW CHALLENGES.
I KNOW WHAT MY VALUES ARE
AND, OF THE DECISIONS I MAKE
I EASILY ACCEPT COMPLIMENTS
AND PRAISE FROM OTHERS.
I TAKE PRIDE IN WHAT I'VE ACCOMPLISHED
AND LOOK FORWARD TO WHAT I INTEND TO
ACHIEVE.
I BELIEVE IN MY ABILITY TO SUCCEED.
I LOVE MYSELF JUST THE WAY I AM.
I DON'T HAVE TO BE PERFECT TO BE LOVED
THE MORE I LOVE MYSELF,
THE MORE I AM ABLE TO LOVE OTHERS.

WHAT I AM LEARNING:

I AM LEARNING TO LOVE MYSELF
MORE EVERY DAY
I AM LEARNING TO BELIEVE IN MY
UNIQUE WORTH AND CAPABILITIES.
I AM LEARNING TO TRUST MYSELF
AND OTHERS.
I AM LEARNING TO RECOGNIZE
AND TAKE CARE OF MY NEEDS.
I AM LEARNING THAT MY FEELINGS AND
NEEDS ARE JUST AS IMPORTANT
AS ANYONE ELSE'S
I AM LEARNING TO ASK OTHERS
FOR WHAT I NEED
I AM LEARNING THAT IT IS OKAY TO SAY NO
TO OTHERS WHEN I NEED TO
I AM LEARNING TO TAKE LIFE
ONE DAY AT A TIME
I AM LEARNING TO APPROACH
MY GOALS ONE DAY AT A TIME.
I AM LEARNING TO TAKE BETTER CARE
OF MYSELF

I AM LEARNING HOW TO TAKE MORE TIME
FOR MYSELF EACH DAY
I AM LEARNING TO LET GO OF DOUBTS AND FEAR.
I AM LEARNING TO LET GO OF WORRY.
I M LEARNING TO LET GO OF GUILT (OR SHAME).
I AM LEARNING THAT OTHERS RESPECT AND LIKE
ME.
I AM LEARNING HOW TO BE MORE
COMFORTABLE AROUND OTHERS.
I AM LEARNING TO FEEL MORE CONFIDENT
IN ___________.(FILL IN)
I AM LEARNING THAT I HAVE A RIGHT TO
______________(specify)
I AM LEARNING THAT IT'S OKAY
TO MAKE MISTAKES.
I AM LEARNING THAT I DON'T HAVE TO BE
PERFECT TO BE LOVED.
I AM LEARNING TO ACCEPT MYSELF
JUST THE WAY I AM.
I AM LOVE
I AM A RADIANT BEING OF LIGHT
I AM A WONDROUS SPIRITUAL BEING
I AM A WONDROUS HUMAN BEING
I AM UNIQUE AND PERFECT INSIDE AND OUT
I AM DESERVING OF LOVE.
I AM WORTHY OF LOVE
I LOVE AND APPRECIATE MYSELF AS I AM.
I AM GETTING BETTER AND BETTER
EVERYDAY IN EVERY WAY.
I AM CONTINUALLY PROJECTING FORTH
LIGHT AND LOVE.
I AM AN OPEN CHANNEL FOR THE
CREATIVE ENERGY OF THIS UNIVERSE.
I AM OPEN TO RECEIVE ALL OF THE
BLESSINGS THIS ABUNDANT UNIVERSE
HAS TO OFFER.
I AM NOW ATTUNED TO THE
PERFECT PLAN OF MY LIFE.

Format your own or select all of the affirmations on the list, put them on individual 3 x 5 file cards. Read through the stack slowly and with feeling once or twice a day. Doing this in front of a mirror is an excellent idea. It is my opinion that self esteem is a gift you give yourself because you owe it to yourself not to sabotage your life. If you do not love and respect yourself no one else can or will. The longing of the human heart to be loved for itself can only be soothed when we learn to love ourselves.

When we truly feel we are a wondrous, Spiritual Beings having a Human experience, our life becomes a daily adventure. Please ask yourself "Do I deserve to love myself?". Any hesitation, or an answer other than a resounding YES indicates that you do not love yourself enough. There can be many reasons for that but often stems from not receiving enough love as a child, even if you had excellent care; it can also stem from spending time in an emotionally abusive relationship which caused your inner self to be out of balance.

When we do not love ourselves enough, we feel that we cannot take good care of ourselves and easily "give our power away" to another; we can feel that only another person or some material thing can make us happy. When we are blessed with that person or material thing, we find that we are still unhappy. If your answer to the question is not a yes, there's work to be done.

Make a commitment now to begin; the work isn't hard, but does require that you do it as often as possible. Reading a set of affirmations is easy. Pick up a cloth bound journal or even a notebook will do to start your own journal of affirmations to be said at least once a day preferably before sleeping; as you refresh your body, refresh your mind.

Please give this self esteem work a full 90 day commitment. It took me 2 years to do the full 90 days; if a day is missed, just start over the next day. You will change how you think about yourself forever.

SELF PITY: Its easy to have a pity party and sometimes misery does love company; don't fall into a trap and get stuck in pitying yourself. All of us get a fair share of pain; pick yourself up, dust off, and begin again! Remember: Today is the first day of the rest of your life!

To Be Your Best Self:
The good you find in others, is in you too.
The faults you find in others, are your faults as well
After all, to recognize something you must know it.
The possibilities you see in others,
are possible for you as well.
The beauty you see around you, is your beauty.
The world around you is a reflection, a mirror
showing you the person you are.
To change your world, you must change yourself.
To blame and complain will only make matters worse.
Whatever you care about, is your responsibility.
What you see in others, shows you yourself.
See the best in others, and you will be your best.
Give to others, and you give to yourself.
Appreciate beauty, and you will be beautiful.
Admire creativity, and you will be creative.
love and you will be loved.
Seek to understand, and you will be understood.
Listen, and your voice will be heard.
Teach, and you will learn.
Show your best face to the mirror, and you'll
be happy with the face looking back at you.
-Author Unknown

I received this verse in email. This was so well written, if anyone knows the author please email Lite@astrongwoman.org to let me know so I may give proper credit in future revisions.

SEX: At its highest and best use it is the expression of the love a couple feels for each other. The joining together of a man and woman for the sake of sharing love, building a life and a family together; the lowest expression, for physical release only, can leave many women and some men too, feeling used. When sex is true love-making it becomes an awesome experience for both parties. We are all born with a sex drive, it is up to each person to manage that sex drive.

It is a must to practice safe sex as a means of preventing unwanted pregnancies, and sexually transmitted disease, which could be permanent and in the case of aides, fatal. Young girls (and some older women too) often have sex and are too embarrassed to talk to the boy or man about protection. If you are old enough to be in an intimate situation then you are old enough to talk about it and should do so for your OWN Protection. Don't just leave it up to the boy or man. So what if he "doesn't like the feel of" the condom? If he isn't willing to protect you and him, then you can believe he wouldn't protect himself with someone else either. That's how sexually transmitted diseases get started. A word of caution: rubbers do break or are put on, or taken off wrong which can still result in pregnancy or disease but your chances are still better.

Write out and practice in the mirror what you will say in advance. This simple step will make it easier to think of what to say should the need arise. Plus you will become more comfortable talking about sex. The best option is to just "say no." Will the boy not like you? Maybe, but if he wants you to do something that you aren't all that willing to do or your parents wouldn't want you to do, then he's just not the right boyfriend for you, no matter how "cute" or "fine" he is. No sex before marriage is still the most favorable idea. In these days of Aids and HIV at epidemic proportions there's a lot to be said for having one partner; there are a few other sexually transmitted diseases that are permanent, but aids can be fatal. No sex until the right partner comes along is way more preferable to "dead."

One major problem many women experience is allowing themselves to enjoy sex, after years of hearing, "nice girls don't," how can they relax and enjoy the experience fully when the time is right? Makes for a lot of ladies who never experience the pleasure of love making; it becomes something they do for their partner. For some, the best they can get out of sex is feeling the closeness of their partner. Some of us just aren't comfortable in our own skin, and are not comfortable or feel shame without clothes.

Remember, love-making between two people who love

each other is a good thing, allow yourself to feel that. Better to be open about sex with your girls and boys; talk about sex as a normal human experience, AND responsibility in personal relationships. Why do we have so many teenage pregnancies? Is it because we were honest and open with our children about sex? I don't think so. I attribute the high teenage birthrate to the fact they are out looking for love they should be getting at home from the family or caretakers.

Please do not tell your daughters or sons that sex is *nasty*. It is not. It is a normal part of life. Why place that burden upon them so that when they are older, they cannot function normally. I have wondered if that is where the masochistic sex comes in. I have never understood mixing pleasure with pain. If you are experiencing any sexual problems in your marriage, seek professional help and remember open, honest, communication is the key. If you are "faking it" to please your partner, please understand you are short changing yourself.

If you typically like the closeness of sex but cannot seem to let go enough to really have a fantastic experience, become open enough with yourself to explore the use of sexual aides available on the market today. I do not believe the old wives tale that masturbation will make you go crazy or somehow depraved. If you are single and of age to be sexually active, exploring masturbation could easily prevent your becoming controlled by good sex with a totally undesirable partner. We do fall "in lust" but that will cool off in time, falling "in love" with a person for who they are is best. Day to day life, babies, and just plain tiredness can also take a toll on passion, don't be embarrassed to talk to your doctor about the loss of passion.

A wondrous Minister, Pastor Pam, explained to a ladies group why we are so vulnerable and why we should protect ourselves until we have the right man: "The way the woman's body is designed, with a man entering inside, leaves us emotionally vulnerable of becoming attached to the man" I believe that to be true so we better darn well have the best partner we can choose. If a man loves you, he will marry you.

Do make sure he's good husband material, love does not change a person only they can change themselves.

What about the people in the world who use sex as a means of controlling another person? Well, we all have an abundance of sexual energy that must be managed to prevent ourselves from becoming enslaved by sexual acts. There are many good sex therapy books out there that offer ways of dealing with that. I do not believe that masturbation makes you crazy, do some research on your own.

After the highly published scandal of a person in high office, it seems that the teenagers and others are having an epidemic of oral sex. I just want to suggest that our genitalia, is where we rid our body of waste. If you are going to consent to oral sex then please know how clean this person is first (I believe that is something we cannot know about another unless we are married to them). Yes, it is a way to prevent pregnancy, it does not prevent the transmission of sexually transmitted diseases (STD), AND puts you in contact with this person's inner most germs, in other words, think long and carefully about what you are doing, and spend some time exploring why; oral sex does prevent pregnancy, but the better option is birth control; engaging in oral sex does not excuse an affair just because there is no genital contact. It is "sex" plain and simple. There is such a thing as sex addiction, please seek therapy if you feel the time devoted to sex, sexual thoughts or various partners could be extreme. See Chapter A—Addiction. M—Morals.

On another note: Once you become a grandparent especially now in the 2000's one has to wonder if the whole world has gone nuts as far as sex goes. With the advent of computers and webcams, a whole new era has exploded, of raw sex in cyberspace. One has to wonder what happened to the term "monogamous", honest, caring relationships with love shared between two people? It

becomes a matter of choice whether one is going to have morals or not. Morals and ethics are cousins, if you don't have either you are living a life that will end in heartbreak and disaster.

Interesting isn't it that men call themselves "Dogs" these days and women refer to themselves as "bitches" (female dog), not to mention all the derogatory lyrics in music that our young people listen to on a daily basis. I find it sad when a show about "desperate" unhappy women finds its way to prime time television and is highly rated. If you watch those women, there are times when they are deliberately cruel and coldhearted to their spouses and others. That makes for serious dysfunction and not the highest and best use of the life, nor for the highest good of the family. Living as a loving, moral and compassionate person is a matter of choice but I promise you if you make that choice for yourself, those in your life circle will be happy people. See Chapters E- Ethics, M—Morals.

SINCERITY: A good quality to cultivate. When you meet up with a sincere, loving person it is so refreshing, and when you leave their presence, you leave feeling good about them and yourself. SINGLE LIVING: Some women and men too will decide that living the single life is best for them. Some of us just cannot seem to find the right partner. If you find yourself living the single life, then be happy about it and set your self up a home that you love. Later on you might change your mind about being single. When a person is comfortable with themselves, being alone is not the scary situation it seems to be. Many single people enjoy active, busy lives and are HAPPY and loving folks.

SINGLE PARENTING: Most of us didn't set out to be single parents, but after a series of life events, death, or just not being able to get along with the other parent, find ourselves alone, facing the awesome task of full responsibility for the children. Most single parents have to counsel themselves constantly so as to not take the worries, anger if any, toward the other parent, out on the children.if there is no other other adult in the home, don't treat them as one and share your burdens over finances or other worries. They are CHILDREN not yet equipped to face adult concerns and it shouldn't be laid on them; when it is their time to face such concerns, they will come and ask how to handle it.

Single parenting well done, carries an awesome reward and blessing. I told my children, we are in this together, it is like a partnership, and we have our responsibilities to each other. These are mine and these are yours, and we talked about what I expected of them, and what they could expect from me. It worked well for me, my children have been my greatest blessing. The single best thing a single parent can do for their child(ren) is to write them love notes; "I love you", "Have a great day" is all they really need to find in their backpack, book, or lunchbox; it reinforces the fact that they are loved. Writing letters to teenagers, allows you to get your point across without back-talk, and they actually *think* about what you are saying. See Chapter A—Abandonment.

Remember I am not talking about notes that berate them, I am talking about notes that build them up, confident that they are cared about; did I write some "you did such and such and I didn't like it" type of letters? Sure I did, but I always stressed that I LOVED them, just didn't like what was going on. Did I get some nasty notes back sometimes? Sure, but at least I knew what they were thinking and Could answer back with what I was thinking. If you have done or said something that you really feel later was overboard, don't ever feel you can't apologize. Children are the most forgiving and they do love their parent(s), not only that but you are teaching them to learn how to apologize. See also Chapters P—Parenting, S—Sex.

SOUL: Since Aristotle in 350 BC, all of the great thinkers have pondered "soul." My version is: Soul is the essence of who we are. The energy moving our body and what will live on after the death of the body; returning to its home in the heavens. We are not meant to fail, and when we transition to the spiritual realms we will get all the philosophical answers that aren't clear now. It is my belief that animals have souls too. When I swat at a bug, I say sorry, "go on to your next life". See Chapters N—Near Death Experience, R—Reincarnation.

SOUL CONTRACT: It is my belief that we meet with heavenly counselors before entering this world, and take a look at what lessons we have completed and those we still need to master. Much like we choose what classes to take in a semester, we choose what lessons we will work on.

SOULMATES: I am not into the hype of today which implies that we have ONE soulmate. It is my belief that all of our friends, family and pets are, our soulmates; To think we have only 1 negates all of our other important relationships. Soulmate relationships are for our growth and that of the other party; they do not always last many years, with some, we would not want them to, for not every soulmate relationship is a "happy" experience, but it teaches one or many lessons.

SPIRITUALITY: A strong spirituality and faith determines the of level of happiness we feel every day; strengthens our coping mechanism as we meet life everyday and is what resonates within us when we are divinely connected to our source. STRENGTH: Not be to confused with physical strength, (although that is a good thing), inner strength is what sustains you on life's journey. Does that mean we never cry? Oh my no! Not at all.

Strength is a gift you give to your loved ones as you hold out your hand compassionately when they stumble. Strength is a covenant you make with yourself, after all, somebody has got to be strong; why not you? STRESS: Stress is anything that keeps you and your spirit in a state of unrest. Worry about everything and/or anything produces a high stress level. Use grounding techniques to quiet the mind and relieve stress. Remember to stop as often as possible in your busy life to have some FUN.

SUBSTANCE ABUSE: Get Help, Get Help, **GET HELP!!!** If you had cancer or some other physical problem you would run to the doctor. This is just as serious AND effects all the people that love you or who you are close to. It could be possible that you are the product of generations of ancestors who also were challenged by substance abuse, understand that it is imperative that you get help for the sake of your own children or other young members of your family circle. Become a role model for them so that if they are challenged and need the strength to break the cycle, they will have the example of someone older in the family who took charge and learned to "just say no" or to say "NO MORE"! See Also Chapter A—Addiction.

SUICIDE: It is my personal belief that many human beings will have thoughts of suicide at least once in their lifetime; occasionally this can happen with very young children, but it is more apt to begin around the time of puberty. The more painful the childhood, the earlier suicidal thoughts will start.

I believe that if more of us really knew and understood Astrology, we would understand that what is so difficult to face will change and have an idea of when. I have always thought that if someone was told, yes, this is a rough time, it will be better in one month (or two or three) we would be better able to cope with rough times, and there would be less suicide in the world.

A Professor of Philosophy told me once, "Suicide is the worst assault on other people". I found that to be true; I do not think a suicidal person sets out to hurt those they love, more, they feel that family would be better off without them, or that it is a way to stop themselves from hurting someone they love.

I DO NOT believe that a person who commits suicide will be banished to the *hell* religions speak of. I believe we have a loving Creator who understands our pain but one who wants us to conquer life's dilemmas; if we cannot, I believe we still go to heaven and will be tended to by loving counsel.

Sometimes a person feels that they have made so many mistakes that they cannot get it right. That is just not the truth. Our "mistakes" are lessons our soul is challenged with in order to grow.

SURVIVOR: We all are survivors of something. You might have survived one experience or many, an abusive childhood or relationship, a rape experience; just about any negative that can happen. You might have had an accident in which you physically survived, when all indications were that you should not have. Yes, we do get second chances. If it is not our *time* no matter what happens to us, we will survive. Obviously, you have a job and living still to do.

SUN CHARGED WATER: You will need 1 gallon per person, per day. Take 1 gallon and place it in the Sun for 3–4 hrs

Take an empty gallon jug and transfer the water back and forth to aureate it, 3 times. If you are very energy sensitive you will notice the energy of this water as you drink it throughout the day. If you do not notice a difference, no problem! You will feel a difference in your vitality within a week. I first read of this in one of Linda Goodman's books.

SURGERY: We are blessed to have the research and medical advances of our doctors; the medical profession is now incorporating "alternative healing" and the title is changing to "Complimentary Healing". It is good that the medical profession is expanding to include spirituality and becoming more broad minded to the fact that other methods are also valid healing modalities.

At some point in our lives, most of us will have had at least one surgery, due to necessity of illness or choice i.e., plastic or cosmetic surgery. Many insurance companies require a 2nd opinion if a surgery is deemed necessary and that is a very good thing. It is my opinion that if a doctor recommends surgery, seek a 2nd opinion, and think long and hard about the surgery (unless it is an emergency).

You will ask be asked to sign a consent form before surgery. Look it over carefully, and if there is some wording that makes you uncomfortable, talk it over with a trusted friend or loved one AND your doctor before signing it.

This is a true story of the Authors personal experience: As a young mother (26 yrs old) with three young children, she became pregnant with the fourth which turned into an ectopic (tubal) pregnancy; that condition is not easily diagnosed (or wasn't in December, 1976); her ob/gyn doctor referred her to a "specialist". He wanted immediate hospitalization for a "test" and possible surgery, so the young mother decided to wait until the day after Christmas to be with her children, son 3, and twin daughters 2. Once in the hospital she was presented with the consent form she was immediately concerned about the wording "possible hysterectomy" the nurse brushed that off as "routine wording"; the mom told the nurse, that she didn't want a hysterectomy unless she agreed with the necessity;

Upon awakening in the recovery room, she'd had a complete hysterectomy which not only removed her uterus, but both ovaries, setting her up for a miserable time "surgical menopause" while having to care for three active toddlers at home; to make matters worse, she became a prime candidate for (and later developed) osteoporosis which one doctor describes like this: "Osteoporosis is a terrible disease".

I do not advocate refusing any help necessary and surgery can save your life, I am pointing out that we have to not be afraid of taking some responsibility in decisions that can leave you forever changed.

Please follow doctors orders after surgery and do not do too much too soon. You might feel great, but if you do not listen to the orders you might pay for that 10 or 20 years down the road. A doctor once told me "every surgery weakens you", so please take good care of yourself!

SYNCHRONICITY: Carl Jung created the term Synchronicity to describe the meaningful coincidences that occur in ones life. When things are "in sync," they are working together properly and in a flow. I welcome Synchronicity in my life and love it when a series of "and then" moments all come together in the proper order just when you need them to. In our busy lives we don't always notice Synchronicity, but if we look back at events we can clearly see just how it seemed to flow right along.

CHAPTER T

Tears, Temptation, Tenacity, Teens, Therapy, Think, Thoughts, Time, Tolerance, Toxins.

TEARS: A gift of our creator to release emotional build up. There is no shame in shedding tears, whether one is male or female. Years back boys and men were taught that it was unmanly to cry. If that was true, boy babies wouldn't be born with tear ducts.

TEMPTATION: The Lord's Prayer says in part "...lead us not into temptation and deliver us from evil". Some religions and cultures believe in satan or evil spirits that will tempt people with an opportunity that winds up being their worst nightmare. We've all heard "If something looks or sounds too good to be true, it probably is", it could just be bad for you. Many things can tempt people, money, sex, power, prestige, legal or illegal drugs, alcohol, food, or all of the above and more. This world offers many things good and not so good; it is up to us to determine what is good for us or what can lead to a disaster and stay away from it. Set and follow a good code of ethics for yourself and you won't go wrong or become en-snarled in something that will take a therapist and a lot of prayer to get you out of.

TEENS: Those wonderful little bundles placed in your arms after a birth, will eventually grow up and become teenagers. Love them and stay as close to them as possible. It is said that teenagers and the elderly are the biggest victims, perhaps because one set (teens) think they know it all and the other set (elderly) have forgotten a lot of the scams they knew about when younger.

No matter what, they deserve and need your love. If they seem to shut you out, write to them, letters not berating them, but telling them of your dreams for them, and how proud you are of them. If they are loved at home, they will not seek out unhealthy forms of love outside of the home; perhaps they might veer off course, but love and reason will bring them back. Do keep an eye on who their friends are. Even rebellious teens find security in knowing their parents love them and while they might act like they don't care for your discipline, and rules, later on, as adults they will come back and tell you how much they appreciated you. The teen years don't last forever and can actually be fun!

TENACITY: If at first you don't succeed, try and try again. There's a lot to be said for children's books, the story of the Little Train chugging up the mountain is a good one, all the while saying: " I think I can, I think I can"...when faced with challenges, keep going, keep improving and before you know it, you WILL. Don't let "I can't do this" be something you dwell on; if you say you can't, you won't.

THERAPY: Too often fear of therapy and therapists or shame that one might need their services, can keep us stuck in the vicious cycle of our fears and issues. Therapists have spent many years of study to prepare to help others work through their issues and live a more fulfilling life. Seeking therapy doesn't mean that we are "crazy" or not as good as other people. It is normal for most of us to have at least one issue during our life that a therapist can help us with. Therapy isn't a "magic pill" nor is there a magic cure. It takes firm inner commitment to want to be well and happy, in order for therapy to be its most effective.

Do not let shame cause you to suffer alone. So what if you have to admit that you made the wrong choice in partners, or have anger, or are just plain unhappy. We are all human and human beings make mistakes, or get on the wrong path. The person who seeks help in spite of embarrassment at admitting what is going on in their life, is the person who will move forward to a vibrantly healthy, and happy life experience.

If your insurance offers several therapists, and you don't like the one assigned or don't seem to resonant with their spirit, don't give up, try another therapist. Get recommendations from friends if at all possible. Shop wisely for the right therapist and ask for a therapist who specializes in what you are dealing with. For instance, if you had a rough childhood, seek out a therapist who specializes in "healing the inner child". Psychiatric Hospitals are very helpful in finding a therapist to match what is going on for you, whether that be anger, inner-child, grief, etc.

It is true that not all therapists are "good" or reputable, they are first of all, human beings. If you begin to suspect that yours is purposely causing you to be dependent upon them, find another one. It is a good idea for the family and friends to monitor a person in therapy. If they appear to be getting worse, ask to meet with their therapist and see how you feel; don't always assume that your loved one is just taking a turn for the worst. If they are taking medications and you notice a drastic change or they are beginning to get more depressed, notify their doctor immediately. You may also want to connect with an Emotional Freedom Technique Practitioner; if you would like to know more about this, feel free to contact the author via email: Lite@astrongwoman.org

THINK: Think things out carefully before you act, you have to live with the results and can spend the rest of your life regretting a decision.

THOUGHT: It is said we only use a small percentage of our brain capability, one thing I have noticed is that many of us do not realize how powerful our thoughts are. Metaphysics teaches us about Universal Thought System.

At the core of this system is a set of laws formed in the spiritual realm; unchangeable and eternal, with no doubt and they are dependable. It doesn't matter what religious belief we adhere to or if we do. "Give and you will receive" is a Universal Law that determines the flow of prosperity in our life.

Thoughts create life experiences, if we constantly tell ourselves "I can't", you will find that you really cannot seem to move past a challenge. I once heard: "If you cannot climb a mountain, go around it!".

If you find that you are constantly feeding yourself negative thoughts, do a "cancel, cancel" and affirm: My Life and Affairs are in Divine Order. Before you know it, they will be. Don't let "stinkin thinkin" rob you of your joy in life.

TIME: As we get older we learn that there is a time for everything; a time to be born, and a time to die, life is the filling in-between. In a fast paced Society we learn to rush or worse, "hurry up and wait", when we've charged ahead only to meet with obstacles or delays we didn't expect. If we did not learn at home how to be gentle with ourselves and have patience, is it any wonder that we develop anxiety attacks?

It is said "time heals all wounds." In a sense it does, but we must understand that we all are unique, and process life events in our own way and in our own time. It is easy to say: "get over it", or, "she/he should have gotten over that by now", instead of being sensitive and tolerant of another person. Just as it takes time to plant seeds and have a garden grow, it takes time to heal wounds or situations, patience and some tolerance is required.

We must understand that our time isn't our Creator's time; no matter how we try to change or hurry an outcome along, it just won't happen until it is the right time. See also Chapters A—Anxiety, G—Grief.

TOLERANCE: Be tolerant, of yourself and others. The childhood pastime of making fun of others, is an awful thing, teach your children to be tolerant of others and do not allow siblings to make unkind comments to each other; it will cut down on the cruelty that goes on daily in our schools and on the playgrounds. Teach Tolerance! It is the way to a peaceful world for generations to come.

It is important for us to be tolerant of ourselves, accept those parts of your body that you dislike, whether that be your nose, ears, or some other part of yourself. You are a unique, wondrous, creation, but you will never feel it unless you see yourself and treat yourself like the Divine Spirit that you are. If there is something about your physical self you absolutely do not like, seek out a reputable plastic surgeon, get a nip or a tuck and, get on with the business of living.

Look for the best in everyone, including yourself and you will learn tolerance. If you weren't taught to be tolerant as a child, you can become a tolerant adult by teaching yourself to be kind. Kindness and Tolerance are related to each other and when a person chooses to be kind and tolerant there is Joy. The natural state of men and woman is joy, ever notice how easily a baby who is well cared for will smile?

TOXINS: There are substances toxic to the body and toxic to the spirit, alcohol and cigarettes are both legal, but toxic to the body. Once you become aware of the Divine Spirit you are, it becomes easier to only put in your system things that are good for you. What made me stop drinking completely was something I once read in a book, author unknown: "Evil Spirits look for inebriated persons to overtake them." Have you ever been completely sober and watched another as they started drinking, notice the change? Ever notice a local liquor store with signs offering "wine & spirits"? I say yikes!

States of mind and some thinking can also be toxic, to you as well as people around you. Be positive and wear your "Grace Face." It is possible for you to be in a toxic relationship, whether that be with family or a loved one. Sometimes we don't realize how differently we feel until we are away from that person. We all have what I call an emotional backpack we carry on our backs (unseen), if there is a lot of baggage, and we meet up with a person who has similar issues, we do what I call "duke it out with our emotional backpacks." If we find ourselves arguing a lot or just in conflict with someone, that relationship either is or soon will become toxic.

If you have experienced a bad relationship in your lifetime (and who among us hasn't)? forgiveness must be a part of the healing process or you will carry toxins such as mistrust into the new relationship without even intending to. See Chapters F—Forgiveness; R—Relationships.

CHAPTER U

Understanding, Users

UNDERSTANDING: Some things we aren't going to understand for many years. Most of us strive to understand what life is all about, some of us don't have a clue and are too afraid to poke around to find out. It is a great gift to have an understanding person in our lives or to be an understanding friend, since all human beings crave love and understanding.

USERS: There are some people (both sexes) that think the world and everyone in it owes them. They will take advantage of your time, kindness and money if you allow them too. See also Chapter F—Frogs

CHAPTER V

Victory, Vitamins

VICTORY: The biggest victory in life is to be happy, all the rest is frosting on the cake. Don't forget to pat yourself on the back for a job well done. You have the power within you to succeed, you weren't born to fail.

VITAMINS: A good multi vitamin is a place to start, but shouldn't be the end of the supplements in your diet. Search out and learn for yourself about which herbs or vitamins can help you maintain optimal health, that includes mental health as well as physical. The fact is we do not get all we need in our food, at least most of us don't. An excellent handbook is Earl Mandell's "Vitamin Bible".

CHAPTER W

Weddings, Weight, Wellness, Whining, Wisdom, Woman, Worry, Wounded.

WEDDINGS: Weddings are beautiful and sacred (often expensive) ceremonies of commitment two people make to each other and their newly formed family. Once a couple decide to marry, the wedding can become the main focus. Make sure you know the person you are agreeing to marry and at least believe you will love him after the honeymoon is over.

I do believe you should plan the wedding of your dreams; understand that some men (majority) won't want to know every little detail and some (minority) will want to be a part of each minute detail. Yours might fall somewhere in-between. If it intimidates him, talk to your friends about the wedding, and just love being together during this truly enchanting time. If it isn't enchanting, you could be headed for disaster later. Don't get caught up in the wedding planning and fail to think about what the marriage will be like. See Chapter M—Marriage.

WEIGHT: It is said that obesity is at epidemic proportions in America. Many people think they cannot lose weight, but the truth is, if we really make up our minds to, we can! Staying motivated is the challenge. Losing weight because someone else wants you to, or because you've met someone new never works, but if we lose it for ourselves because we want to, look our best, we can lose it and keep it off too. There are many good programs and websites for those who want to lose weight. Find the one that is right for you. The same applies for those who want to gain weight.

WELLNESS: To be vibrantly healthy is such a good feeling. Taking responsibility for your own health is a very wise move. For too many generations, physicians have been treated as "gods" and people have taken their word on treatment. There is nothing wrong with researching a condition and really openly talking to your doctor about it. If your doctor won't discuss your condition with you, find another who will. There are many good doctors available who are interested in their patients are human beings. We are a "quick-fix" society, trained to take a pill for this or that; research the meds, and see if you really want to face the side effects that can come with it.

It's perfectly okay to get the diagnosis, and research vitamins or herbal remedies, many work well! Does that mean we should shun treatment? No! I am not saying that at all, just don't be afraid to find out more and see if there are natural remedies. Don't be afraid to get a 2nd opinion. For 5 years, my left foot was very swollen, the doctors didn't know the cause, and prescribed water pills. After some research, I found that the herb, Cayenne, helps the arteries. I bought some, put it in capsule form, to my complete amazement, three months later my foot was no longer swollen. I am very grateful!

WHINING: Children learn quickly that whining can get them what they want. Some people never leave that childish trait behind as they grow up; not much to be said for a 40 year old whiner.

WISDOM: Some old souls are born wise, for the vast majority of us, wisdom comes with age, training and lifestyle. A wise woman is a joy to behold and a wonder to be around. ANY ONE can become a wise woman, all that is needed is the desire to be our best! A good amount of intelligence does not always mean we are wise or have good common sense. I like to say: "I prayed for Wisdom, boy did I get it"! The truth is, wisdom comes as we mature, but we do need to pay attention.

WOMEN: Are the backbones of the home, and family. Many brave ladies joined the Women's Movement and paved the way for us; as a result, many of us are coming into our own and feeling good about being a woman. In many countries, women are still living very difficult lives under men who treat them worse than animals. If you have some extra time, volunteer for whatever Woman's Group appeals to you, and help others to come into their own. Giving back and reaching a hand out to others is always a good idea, and to the recipient, often a welcome relief.

WORRY: Some of us are "worry warts," if we don't have something to worry about, we'll find something. Worry causes us to feel stress, and we all know that stress can bring about ill health. Faith is the antidote to worry, strengthen yours. (see Chapter F, Faith).

WOUNDED: If you have been abused or hurt in any way, you have been wounded. Wounds don't "stuff" away well. They build scar tissue, and will fester underneath the surface of your life and relationships. There is too much talk of forgiving and "forgetting" we do not forget! But we can remember the incident or person, without anger or pain. The BOTTOM LINE to all of our aches and pains is forgiveness.(please see Chapter F, Forgiveness).

CHAPTER X

Xmas, Xylophone,

XMAS: My daughter Kathleen, (who I am sure is a Minister in training), pointed out to me during the Christmas 2004 season: "Mom, did you ever notice that Christmas is abbreviated X-Mas? What they've done is x'ed out Christ from Christmas!" That made plenty of sense to me; please don't X out Christ from your life. We have been blessed with many master teachers and saints, wise are the ones who learn from their example.

XYLOPHONE: My brother Michael said: "Life is like a Xylophone, sometimes when you play it, its sweet and harmonious; other times it sounds awful, awkward and heavy, in other words, it sucks"! Does that mean that it will stay tough? No! Our life cycles, we go up and down. The good thing about sharing with others though, is that we are all not down at the same time and can pick each other's spirits up. Remember, laughter is the best medicine!

CHAPTER Y

Yoga

YOGA: Yoga helps integrate, Mind, Body and Spirit. Beginning Yoga isn't too strenuous, and can be learned in a class setting, or in the privacy of your home via video tapes. Its also an excellent form of exercise with a huge pay-back!

CHAPTER Z

Zipper

ZIPPER: Zipper your lip! The phrase "bite your tongue" applies here. It has been said:"People will forget what you do, but will remember what you say". There truth in that. Ever heard: "You catch more flies with honey than you do with salt?" It means the sweeter you say something the more cooperation you get."

There are times when we just have to get control of what comes out of our mouth. Words and names can cut others like a knife and wound their Spirit, especially in the case of children. We can never look at a person and tell how very sensitive they are.

If someone tells you something in confidence, make sure that you do not share that confidence with anyone, even if you think they do not know who you are talking about. The world is actually smaller than it seems and they could wind up meeting each other later.

I received this poem via email. Although it is entitled Strong Woman, I believe it would apply if written for a Strong Person!

Strong Woman

A strong woman works out every day to keep her body in shape
but a woman of strength kneels in prayer to keep her soul in shape
A strong woman isn't afraid of anything but a woman
of strength shows courage in the midst of her fear
A strong woman won't let anyone get the best of her
but a woman of strength gives the best of herself to everyone
A strong woman makes mistakes and avoids the same in the future
but a woman of strength realizes life's mistakes can also be
God's blessings & capitalizes on them
A strong woman walks sure-footedly but a woman
of strength knows God will catch her when she falls
A strong woman wears the look of confidence on her face
but a woman of strength wears grace
A strong woman has faith that she is strong enough for the journey
but a woman of strength has faith
that it is in the journey that she will become strong.
(Author Unknown)

Recommended Reading

Terri Lynn Taylor
"Messengers of Light"
"Guardians of Hope"
These two books are all about Angels and how to develop a personal relationship with them.
Barbara D'Angeles, Ph.D
"Are You The One for Me?"
Dr. Philip Mac Graw
"Relationship Rescue"
"Life Strategies"
"Family First"

Recommended Websites:

RainbowAura Healing Arts
wwwlovespirit.net
Lynn Andrews
http://www.lynnandrews.com
Medicine Garden
http://www.medicinegarden.com/
Caroline Myss Ph.D.
http://www.myss.com/
Course In Miracles
http://www.acim.org/
Trivita Products
http://www.trivita.com/products.asp
Patricia Lite Hickman
www.astrongwoman.org

ABOUT THE AUTHOR

Patricia Hickman is known to her clients and spiritual family as Lite. Psychic and clairaudient, Lite is a healer and Reiki practitioner (RM), a minister as well as an expert in the field of metaphysics. Lite credits a near death experience (NDE) at age 25 with her spiritual awakening, giving her a glimpse of life beyond death.

Lite's NDE was the motivation for her quest to find deeper meaning and understanding about the soul's journey. Lite has studied various metaphysical disciplines including astrology, tarot, psychic phenomena, spirit release therapy and more. Lite has over 25 years of knowledge and experience gained on this life path and works professionally as a teacher, healer and counselor.

Common Sense For The Soul is a practical guide to life's challenges and changes based on Lite's personal experiences and knowledge of that which is unseen and often misunderstood. Lite loves to counsel and help others, teaching metaphysical techniques and principles that can help you overcome obstacles and restore balance and peace to your days. When not counseling others, Lite is devoted to her family of three children and nine grandchildren and resides in Milwaukee, Wisconsin.

For information on readings or to contact Lite, please visit:
http://www.astrongwoman.org

19053437R00118

Made in the USA
Lexington, KY
04 December 2012